Contents

Introduction

When I was asked by CICO to write my first book, *Quilting Basics*, I tried to lay out the lessons in a way that I would want to be taught if I was starting as a new quilter. We started with simple techniques and worked to more and more complex examples of quilting. Quilting was not something I really saw as my future; it was something I liked to do because I am a "maker." I like to make all sorts of things, but it turns out I have a knack for quilting—so here we are today, trying to explain what I do. My many years working in children's publishing, designing and engineering pop-up books, led me to a fundamental skill of arranging shapes and color. Using math and measurements to get pop-ups to function is essential and I was able to bring that meticulousness to my designs and templates.

Then I was contacted by the great team at CICO asking if I would be interested in working on a second book. I thought it would be a great chance to incorporate new little tricks and skills I have continued to learn and share them in a second lesson book, but that was not what they wanted to do—I was told that I could do whatever I wanted and was free to design as I saw fit. Hearing that puts a smile on your face—it makes you feel like people appreciate what you create. Then came the daunting task of designing and making 25 projects! Some people don't come close to making 25 projects in a year, but I needed to design and make 25 in just a few months. That was not an easy task by any stretch of the imagination, and imagination was what was needed.

I sat and started to plan the 25 projects and soon realized that I was trying to be too far out there. I needed to simplify my mind and get back to what I like to do: take bold geometric shapes and patterns and add them to my love of color. I have always loved color—my first car was a bright yellow 1971 VW Beetle—so why would I shy away from that? Once I started making the first project, the second one was already being designed in my head. The process started to flow from one to another, and before I knew it I had 25 original designs in front of me. Then began the hard part of writing down what I do in my head so easily, so that others could take their own favorite fabrics and make amazing versions of my designs. That is really what it is all about: being able to share what I have learned, figuring out for myself alternative ways to tackle what I have feared and passing this on to others.

Over the last five to six years I have been really lucky to meet so many great people in the quilting world who are extremely supportive and have welcomed me with open arms into their tight-knit community. They are always willing to lend materials to my craft, which allows me to continue to design without worry. I look forward to continuing our friendship—and to those whom I don't know yet, that will soon change!

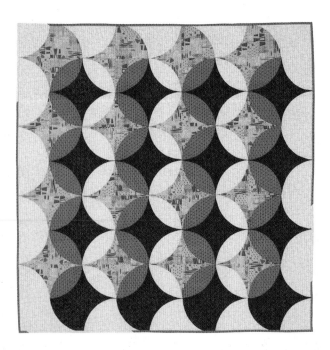

modern QUILTING

modern QUILTING

25 step-by-step projects for cool and contemporary patchwork and quilts

MICHAEL CAPUTO

CICO BOOKS

LONDON NEW YORK

The measurements in this book are given in both imperial and metric. Please follow one system throughout and do not mix the two.

Published in 2018 by CICO Books
An imprint of Ryland Peters & Small Ltd
20–21 Jockey's Fields, London WC1R 4BW
341 E 116th St, New York, NY 10029

www.rylandpeters.com

10 9 8 7 6 5 4 3 2 1

A CIP catalog record for this book is available from the Library of Congress and the British Library.

ISBN: 978-1-78249-641-0

Printed in China

Editor: Marie Clayton
Designer: Alison Fenton
Photographer: Emma Mitchell
Illustrator: Stephen Dew
Layout diagrams and templates:
Michael Caputo
Stylist: Nel Haynes

In-house editor: Anna Galkina
Art director: Sally Powell
Head of Production: Patricia Harrington
Publishing manager: Penny Craig
Publisher: Cindy Richards

TECHNIQUES—Basic kit

When you start quilting, you don't have to go out and buy every tool ever made. A few essentials are all you need. You can add specialty tools as you progress and grow. This is what I suggest you have as a basic kit.

Sewing machine

This is probably the most expensive part of sewing and quilting. If you are a beginner, you don't need to splurge on a super-pricey machine with thousands of options. Choose a machine that fits your budget and will allow you to adjust the needle position left and right. Look for a well-equipped sewing machine with a few basic decorative stitches. If you can find one that has a needle down function, get it. Your machine can be manual or digital.

¼-in (6-mm) foot
Using this foot will help you sew seams that are a consistent ¼in (6mm) in width, which is a must in patchworking.

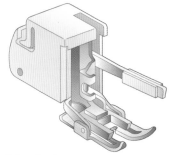

Walking foot
Also known as an even feed foot, this specialist foot is a must for any quilter. Just as the feed dogs on the machine pull the fabric from the bottom, a walking foot pulls the fabric from the top. When you are working with thicker materials, this will help to eliminate uneven stitching.

Zipper foot
Perfect for installing a zipper into fabric, this foot can be used on either the right or left side of the needle and allows extremely close stitching without hitting the teeth on the zipper.

Essentials

Quilter's pins (or glass-headed straight pins) and a pincushion: Quilter's pins are long thin pins with a plastic flower head for easy grabbing. Glass-headed straight pins are great if you need to press while your pieces are pinned. Don't press when using quilter's pins, as the plastic heads will melt.

Curved or straight safety pins: With curved safety pins, you can easily scoop the three layers of your quilt sandwich when basting (tacking). The straight version works just as well, but requires a bit more fiddling.

Iron and ironing board: Essential for pressing your seams correctly. Your household iron will do just fine—there is no need for a special iron as long as it has a steam function.

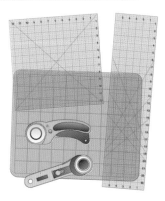

Rotary cutter, self-healing cutting mat, and quilter's rulers: Rotary cutters come in different sizes—25mm, 45mm, and 90mm. The 45mm cutter is a great universal size for quilting. Opt for a cutter with automatic safety guard. Use your cutter with a quilter's ruler on a self-healing cutting mat to cut precisely measured fabric units. To begin with, I recommend that you buy a 6 x 24-in (15 x 60-cm) ruler for cutting fabric from the bolt and a 12½-in (32-cm) square ruler for making sure your blocks are trimmed square and ready for assembly. You can get more rulers as you need them.

Fabric scissors (large and small): It is best to have 8-in (20-cm) scissors for more general cutting like circles or appliqué shapes. Small scissors are great for snipping loose threads. Never use your fabric scissors to cut paper, as this will blunt the blades.

Hand sewing needles: "Sharps" are the standard quilting needle. They come in a variety of lengths and points, and are perfect for hand piecing and attaching binding.

Seam ripper: A small seam ripper usually comes with your sewing machine, but if it does not this piece of kit should be number 1 on your list. The sharp point allows you to glide under a tight stitch while the blade breaks the thread.

Quilter's pen or pencil: There are dozens of different pencils and pens used in quilting. Soft pencils allow for the transfer of templates and patterns to the wrong side of the fabric. A chalk

[...] o draw a line on the right side of your [...] brush off, so be careful. A water- or air- [...] sharp lines and will disappear either with [...] the air.

[...]g): If you are patchworking in 100 percent [...] should use a 100 percent cotton batting—or [...] new cotton/bamboo blends—so that they wash and dry in the same fashion. There are different thicknesses of batting; the higher the loft, the thicker the batting. Lower loft means a thinner weight. Thicker-weight batting will make machine quilting more difficult. Choose whatever works for your project.

Threads: I also like to use 100% cotton threads when working on my projects. For the majority of my piecing I use a white thread, as it is neutral and will work with a variety of colors.

Fabrics for quilting

Choosing fabrics for your quilts can be both stressful and enjoyable; there are so many options that your head will spin. So how can you make sense of it all?

Types of fabric

I prefer to use 100% cotton fabrics whenever possible, the higher the thread count, the better your end product will be. Although bolts of fabric do not specify the thread count, you can easily tell if it is a good weight cotton with a higher than normal thread count by holding an open section up to the light. If you can see through it very easily, then you have a loose-weave fabric that should be avoided. The fibers will break down faster and your heirloom quilt will not make it past a few washings.

Buying fabric

The traditional way of buying fabric is from the bolt, and most patchwork cotton fabrics are 44in (112cm) wide. Bolts come in two basic lengths, a 7-yard (approx. 6.5-meter) bolt and a 15-yard (approx. 13.7-meter) bolt. That means the roll on display will be that length by 44in (112cm) wide and will be folded in half, from selvage to selvage. You can also buy pre-cut pieces in a range of different sizes for quilting. But even if you're used to buying fabric for dressmaking or home-furnishing projects, the terminology associated with quilting fabrics can be confusing to start with. So what does it all mean?

Fat quarters and fat eighths

Normally when you go into a fabric store and ask for ¼yd or ¼ metre of fabric, the assistant will unroll some fabric from the bolt, measure 9in or 25cm down the length, and cut across the whole width, giving you a piece that measures 9in high x 44in wide (or 25 x 112cm in metric measurements). This is a "long quarter."

A "fat quarter" means that you start with a yard or meter of the fabric, fold it in half both horizontally and vertically, and then cut it into four along the fold lines—so you end up with a piece measuring 18in high x 22in wide (or 50 x 56cm). The total area of fabric is the same as that of a long quarter—but instead of a long, thin strip, you have an off-square shape, which is a much better shape from which to cut smaller squares and triangles.

A "fat eighth," not surprisingly, is half of a fat quarter, and measures 9in (25cm) high by 22in (56cm) wide. Quilting stores generally sell pre-cut quarters, but always check whether the "quarter" that you're buying is fat or long!

Layer cakes are also bundles of square pieces—but they are 10in (25cm) square.

Jelly rolls are individual strips measuring 2½ x 44in (6 x 112cm).

Cutting

Patterns for blocks can require several different size pieces of fabric. The best way to make sure that everything is the size it needs to be is to carefully measure and cut your fabric, using a quilter's ruler and a rotary cutter.

Squaring up

Squaring up your fabric is a very important part of becoming an accurate and precise quilter. When you buy fabric from a shop or online, it will never be 100 percent square—especially if you use fat quarters. Starting with a squared-off corner will ensure your cuts are as precise as possible.

1 Press all your fabrics with a hot iron; this will ensure more accurate cutting.

2 Position your fabric right side up in front of you on a cutting mat, with a selvage edge at the top of the mat. Place your quilter's ruler toward the right side of the fabric, making sure that a little of the fabric sticks out to the right of the ruler. This side may not be straight. Align one of the horizontal marks on the ruler with the selvage. This will ensure that, when you cut off the excess fabric in the next step, you will end up with a perfect 90-degree corner.

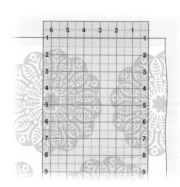

3 With your left hand, press down firmly on the ruler. With your right hand, press down firmly on the rotary cutter and, starting nearest your body, push the cutter away from you through the fabric. This is known as "squaring up."

Cutting fabric patches

Once you have squared up the edge, you can begin to measure and cut your fabric into pieces of the required size.

1 With your ruler right side up in front of you, identify the size you need to cut. Here we are cutting 4½-in (11.5-cm) strips from a fat quarter. If you are right handed, turn the fabric so that the squared cut that you made in step 3 of Squaring Up is on the left-hand edge. Position the vertical 4½-in (11.5-cm) rule marks on your ruler along this edge. Use the horizontal line to double check the squareness of the corner.

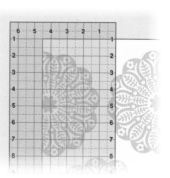

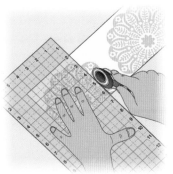

2 With your left hand, press down firmly on the ruler that is covering the width of the strip. With your right hand, firmly press down on the rotary cutter and, in one movement, starting nearest your body, push the cutter away from you through the fabric. Try not to pull the cutter back and forth, as this can cause frayed edges.

3 After the 90-degree corner has been created you can now subcut the strip into smaller sections. Line up the ruler over the fabric the desired width (here we're cutting 4½-in (11.5-cm) squares) and cut as before until you have all the pieces for either your block or your quilt top.

Using a rotary cutter safely

- The blades on the rotary cutter are extremely sharp, so pay close attention to the position of the blade when picking it up off the table.
- Some cutters have automatic safety covers. Some don't! If your blade has a manual cover, be sure to use it and to cover the blade when it is not in use.
- Always cut away from your body and, whenever possible, use a quilter's ruler. The ruler will act as an additional safety barrier and help keep the fabric from shifting when you are cutting.

- Use a self-healing cutting mat. This will help prevent the blade from becoming dull too quickly and stop it destroying your table.
- Apply even pressure and try not to move the blade back and forth.
- It's not pizza! Stand up and, with your ruler firmly in place, guide the blade along the edge in one even cut.
- When changing the blade, carefully unscrew the holder and remove the blade. Whenever possible, place some masking tape around the old blade to help shield the razor's edge.

Half square triangles (HSTs)

The individual method

This method works best when you want all of your finished blocks to have different fabrics. Two squares of contrasting fabrics are cut in half diagonally to give two right-angle triangles in each fabric. To form the square, contrasting triangles are then stitched together along the diagonal, using a ¼-in (6-mm) seam allowance. When you stitch the two triangles together, you lose ¼in (6mm) of each fabric in the seam allowance, so the stitched square will end up smaller than the ones you initially cut. Here's how to get around the problem.

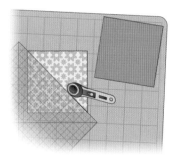

1 Add ⅜ in (1 cm) to the finished size of block that you need. For example, if you are looking to create 2½-in (6.5-cm) blocks, cut two squares each measuring 2⅞in (7.5cm). Using your rotary cutter and ruler, cut both the squares in half diagonally.

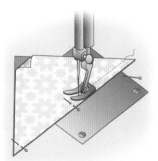

2 Place one triangle from each fabric right sides (RS) together and stitch along the diagonal, using a ¼-in (6-mm) seam allowance.

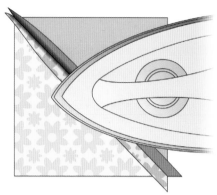

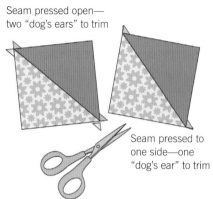

Seam pressed open—
two "dog's ears" to trim

Seam pressed to
one side—one
"dog's ear" to trim

3 Press the stitching line to "set" the stitches, then open out the square and press the seam either toward the darker fabric or open if you will be attaching more HST blocks. Then press the square again from the right side. After pressing, you will have a finished block that is 2½in (6.5cm) square.

4 If you press the seams open, you will need to trim off the little "dog's ears" of fabric that stick out at each end of the diagonal seam on both sides. If you press the seam toward the darker fabric, there will be only one "dog's ear" to trim off on each side.

The double method
Using this method will give you two identical HST blocks.

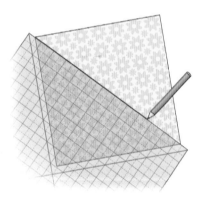

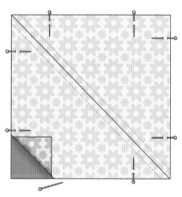

1 First, decide on the finished size you need for your HST blocks. Add ⅞in (22mm) to determine the trim size of your squares. For a 6-in (15-cm) finished block, for example, cut two squares measuring 6⅞in (17.2cm). On the wrong side of one of the blocks, draw one diagonal line from corner to corner with a quilter's pencil or a regular pencil.

2 Pin the two squares RS together, with the pencil line facing you. Using a scant ¼-in (6-mm) seam allowance, sew a parallel line along both sides of the pencil line. Remove the pins.

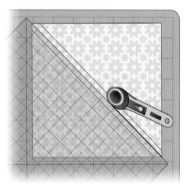

3 Using your rotary cutter and ruler, cut along the pencil line to create two matching HST blocks.

4 Press the HST blocks, following the instructions in step 3 of the Individual Method. Trim off the "dog's ears."

The four-block method

While this method yields the largest number of blocks in one go, it also leaves you with some raw bias edges—so be very careful when handling the blocks so that you don't stretch them out of shape.

1 Multiply the finished size by 0.64 and add that number (rounding up to the nearest ¼ in /5 mm) to the original size (see examples, above). Cut one square of each fabric to this size.

2 Pin the two squares right sides together. Taking a ¼-in (6-mm) seam allowance, sew along all four sides of the squares. It may look like you have done something wrong, but don't worry. Remove the pins.

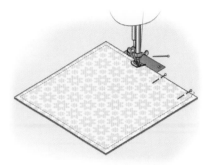

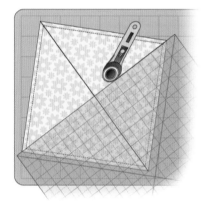

3 Using your rotary cutter and ruler, carefully cut diagonally from corner to corner. Then rotate the mat and cut the opposite diagonal. This will give you four matching HST blocks. Because you have cut on the diagonal, you have created a bias edge—so when handling the blocks try not to stretch them. As you have added a bit to the overall size, you might need to trim the HSTs to the final desired size.

4 Press the HST blocks, following the instructions in step 3 of the Individual Method (see opposite). Trim off the "dog's ears."

Quarter square triangle

Another very common patchwork block that uses squares cut into triangles is the quarter square triangle block. This is made up of two squares sewn together and cut in two ways. Start with two squares at least 1 in (2.5 cm) larger then the finished size you need.

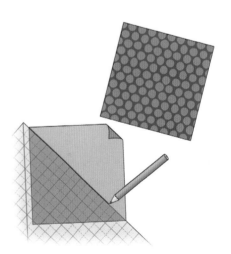

1 For a 5-in (12.5-cm) finished block, you will need to start with two 6-in (15-cm) squares in contrasting fabrics. As in the Double Method for HSTs (see opposite), draw a single diagonal line on the back of your squares.

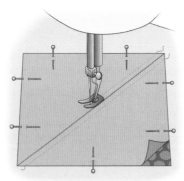

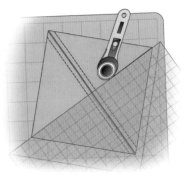

2 Pin the two squares RS together. Sew diagonally across the squares, ¼in (6mm) from each side of the drawn line.

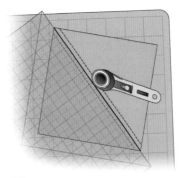

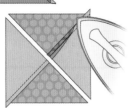

3 Cut along the line, using a rotary cutter and quilter's ruler. Do NOT move the two pieces. Rotate the ruler and cut diagonally across from corner to corner.

4 Open the squares out and press the seams toward the darker fabric. Re-arrange the pieces in squares so that the colors alternate.

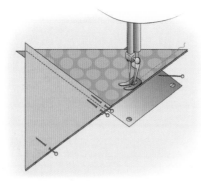

5 Place two pieces RS together, aligning the center seam and nesting the join (see page 17). Pin along the edge to be sewn. Carefully position the piece in your machine and sew using a ¼-in (6-mm) seam allowance.

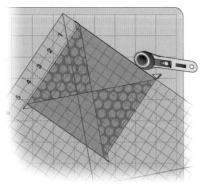

6 Using the marks on your quilter's ruler, find the 2½-in (6-cm) point and place it over the center point where the four fabrics meet. Trim away the tiny bit of excess fabric and repeat on the other three sides, squaring the block wherever possible.

Fussy cutting

Fussy cutting involves cutting out units around a specific part or motif in a printed fabric. For the example in the illustration here, you fussy cut the seven small squares that have a circle at their center.

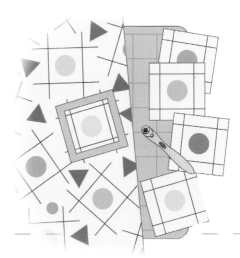

How to use templates

Making re-usable templates

Follow these simple steps to make sturdy templates that you can use time and time again. Paper is not ideal as it's too thin—you can't make multiple tracings without the shape changing slightly each time. Thicker materials such as cardstock or the inside of a cereal box make tracing easier. The most durable template is template plastic, which is available online and from specialist craft and quilting stores. All the templates on pages 118–125 already have the seam allowance included (illustrated by a dashed line on the template), so you won't need to worry about adding it.

1 If you are using a template for a pattern, either scan it into your computer or take it to a photocopy shop.

2 Print or photocopy the template onto cardstock, leaving plenty of space to fold the template and get two pieces. I find that a slightly thicker cardstock is easier to use than plain printer paper—but if that's all you have, paper will work, too.

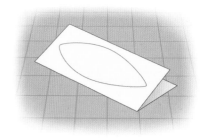

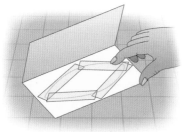

3 On the wrong side of the print-out or photocopy, apply glue or double-sided tape on the inside of the shape.

4 Fold the paper back in half, pressing firmly to join the two pieces. Only one side needs to have the template outline.

5 Using a sharp craft knife on a cutting mat or a pair of scissors, cut along the line. Taking your time and cutting carefully will ensure a properly fitting template.

6 You now have an extra-thick template that is perfect for tracing multiple patterns without any change of shape.

Transferring templates onto fabric

Knowing which side to trace your template can be confusing, but if you labeled them properly when you made them it will be much easier. To transfer them to the fabric, you will need a marker and sharp fabric scissors to cut the shapes out.

Place the template on the right side of the fabric. As you will be drawing the cutting line, you can use a pen, or a quilter's pen or pencil. Draw around the template, then cut on the line as best you can with sharp fabric scissors. If you are tracing the stitching line, it's better to trace it onto the wrong side (WS) of the fabric—but be sure to flip the template before you do so, so that the shape will be the right way round when you cut it out of the fabric.

Piecing

Consistent seams

Setting your machine up to sew a perfect ¼-in (6-mm) seam is crucial to patchworking. In a row of 20 blocks there will be 18 seams, and if each seam allowance is off by just ⅟₁₆in (1.5mm), the row will be either larger or smaller by more than 1in (almost 3cm). When you understand why proper seam allowances are important and can set up your machine for consistent ¼-in.(6-mm) seams, you will be on your way to easy quilting.

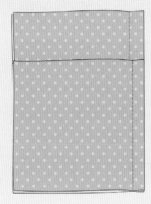

Method 1: Dedicated ¼-in (6-mm) foot

Different brands have different styles of a ¼-in (6-mm) foot. Some are simply just smaller in width then your standard foot and will measure ¼in (6mm) from the needle to the right (and/or left) edge of the foot. Some will have a side guide. Either will work and help you with your consistent seams. To test the accuracy of the foot, line up your fabric edge with the right-hand edge of the foot, then stitch as normal; the seam allowance should be very close to ¼in (6mm). Stitch a few inches, then remove the fabric from the machine and measure the seam allowance using your quilter's ruler. If necessary, make a very slight adjustment by either positioning the fabric just a few millimetres to the right or left of the foot edge or using the needle adjustment settings on your machine. Run another sample and re-measure until you've got it absolutely right.

What is a "scant" ¼-in (6-mm) seam allowance?

This simply means a thread or two smaller than ¼in (6mm)—the exact measurement would be very difficult to measure. Adjust your needle or tape guide to be slightly smaller.

¼-in (6-mm) seam allowance

scant ¼-in (6-mm) seam allowance

Method 2: Standard foot and tape guide

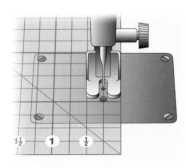

1 Place a quilter's ruler under the presser foot of your machine and slowly wind the needle down by hand so that it almost touches the ruler. Align ¼-in (6-mm) marks on the ruler under the needle.

2 Place a small strip of painter's tape, masking tape, or some post-it notes along the edge of the ruler. Lift the presser foot and carefully remove the ruler from under the needle. When you sew, align the right-hand edge of the fabric with the edge of the tape or post-it notes.

Pressing seams to one side

In quilting, you normally press seams to one side—traditionally toward the darker fabric. This helps eliminate the problem of a dark-colored seam allowance being visible through a lighter-colored fabric. If you are pressing fabrics that are similar in tone, it's good to keep the direction consistent; in other words, always press them either to the right or to the left.

Pressing seams open

In some cases—for example, where adjacent Half Square Triangles come together at the same point—it may be best to press your seams open to distribute the bulk of the fabric and avoid a lump on the finished side. The project instructions in this book will tell you when to press your seams open.

Perfect piecing

It's surprisingly easy to get your patchwork pieces in the wrong order! Work out your fabric placement first by laying out all the pieces on a large, flat surface. Then stack all the pieces for each row in a pile in sewing order—you may find it helps to add a label to each piece, giving the row and piece number: so 1/1 would mean row 1, first piece; 1/2 would mean row 1, second piece, and so on. You could also add the letter "T" for "top," for example, to indicate the direction of the print.

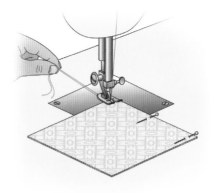

Place the first two pieces RS together and pin if necessary. Carefully place the pieces under the presser foot and, while holding the top and bobbin threads out the back of the machine, begin stitching. Your stitch length should be around 2.5mm. Repeat the process until each row is complete.

"Nesting" seams

Joining rows together can be tricky, as you will have several seams to align. It's a good habit to start your pinning at the center of the row and work outward, first to one side and then the other, pinning at every junction point and in between if you

need to. Starting at one side and working all the way across to the other may leave you with a big discrepancy when you get to the end. Starting in the middle will help if you find that you need to ease (stretch or shrink) the seams to match.

All seams pressed to the left

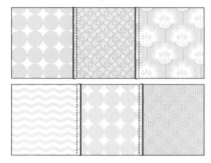

All seams pressed to the right

I The best method is to press the seam allowances on all the odd rows in one direction and all the even rows in the opposite direction.

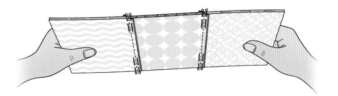

2 Place two rows RS together, taking care to line up the seams carefully. On each side of the seam, insert a pin that goes through all layers, including the pressed seam allowances. This will stop the seam allowances from slipping out of position while you sew, which would create unsightly lumps and bumps in your quilt top and might even mean that the pieces don't align properly. This process is called "nesting."

Chain piecing

Chain piecing is the continuous sewing of blocks or units without breaking the thread. Here, we're sewing a white sashing (dividing) strip to the right-hand edge of 9-patch blocks, but the same method can be used for any repeated units to speed things up. Simply place the two pieces together as you would normally do, and sew off the block at the end. Do not break the thread. Take the two pieces and begin sewing again as you would normally. Once you have finished sewing, you can break the thread and snip between each block. Chain piecing makes a repetitive sequence faster.

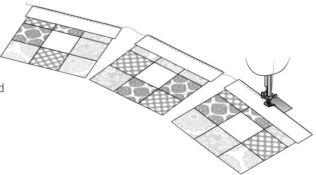

Quilting

Preparing your quilt sandwich

The first thing you need to do is assemble the different layers of your quilt—backing fabric, batting (wadding), and quilt top—and make sure that these layers don't slip out of position when you begin quilting. There are several ways to do this. You can spray baste your layers (using a thin layer of spray glue to temporarily hold your layers for quilting) or thread baste (using basting/tacking stitches through the layers), but I like to pin the layers together using curved quilter's safety pins. Straight safety pins are absolutely fine to use, too; I just prefer the slight curve in the lower pin arm, as it allows you to easily scoop the layers.

Piecing fabric for the backing

Whenever possible, try to find an extra-wide fabric for the backing. They may be hard to come by, so for a full-size quilt you will often need to join several pieces together. I like to piece different color fabrics for backings. Why should the front get all the glory?! As a general rule, I piece backings for small quilts (36–60in/90–150cm) horizontally, with the seams running across the quilt, and backings for larger quilts (over 60in/150cm) vertically.

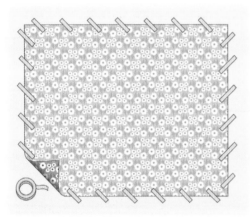

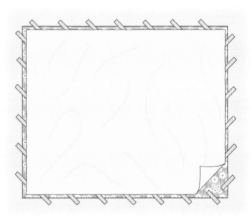

1 To achieve the best outcome, you need to have everything as flat and smooth as possible. Press your backing fabric as flat as you can and place it on a large, flat surface, with the right side facing down. Using masking or low-tack painter's tape, tape down the edges of the quilt backing, smoothing out the wrinkles as you go. Your backing fabric should be about 2in (5cm) larger than the finished quilt top on all sides: if your top measures 64 x 86in (162 x 218cm), for example, then your backing should be a minimum of 68 x 90in (172 x 228cm).

2 With the backing fabric taped to the table or floor, place the batting (wadding) on top, centering it as best you can. Smooth out all the wrinkles, feeling through the batting to the backing. The batting should be 1in (2.5cm) larger on all sides then the top. Tape it down as best you can.

3 Place the quilt top right side up on top, centering it as best you can. Smooth out all the wrinkles, again making sure you feel nothing on the other layers. While you are doing all the smoothing, you should be planning your quilting. This will help you with the positioning of the pins.

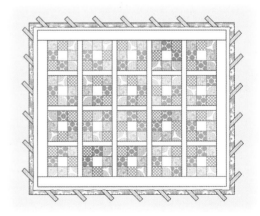

4 Starting at the center of the quilt top, place a safety pin through all layers. Work your way left and right of the center pin, spacing the pins about a palm's width apart, until you reach the edges. Move back to the middle and then pin the next "row," smoothing as you pin. The goal is to have enough pins that, when you push the quilt through your machine, you will not have to worry about anything moving between the layers. Once you have pins all over the quilt, you are ready for the next step—quilting!

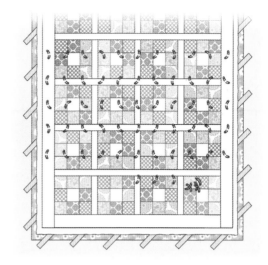

Straight-line quilting

Stitching either vertically or horizontally across the entire quilt gives an interesting texture. This method is simple to do, as you start and finish stitching off the quilt top so you will not have any threads to tie off and bury in the batting (wadding). You can create a different look by using a variegated thread, or even a selection of colors, for your quilting thread. Varying the distance between the rows also adds a different look. Pick a starting point near the middle of the quilt. Work your way in one direction and then go in the other direction when you have reached the end. The more densely quilted you make your quilt, the stiffer it will be.

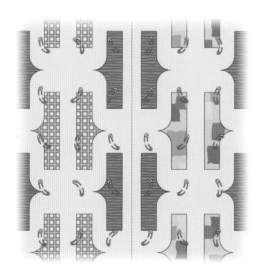

1 Prepare your "quilt sandwich" as described opposite. Start near the center of the quilt and quilt one row, either vertically or horizontally depending on your design.

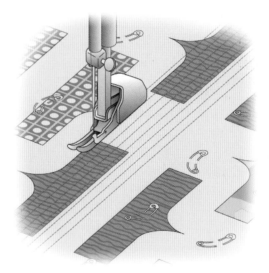

2 Work outward from the center row, quilting first to the left and then to the right of it, using the side of your walking foot as a guide so that the rows are evenly spaced. When you have finished quilting, remove all the safety pins.

Echo quilting

Echo quilting is a very simple method where you use the width of your walking foot as a guide to space the quilting lines. As the name suggests, echo quilting involves stitching concentric lines, each one following the previous one. It can be used to quilt around a motif such as a star. Alternatively, you can stitch curves or simple shapes such as triangles. As long as each line follows the previous one, you can call it echo quilting.

Spirals and curves

To echo a curve or a spiral, you will need to locate your desired starting point on your quilt. I like to start my spiral about a quarter of the way down from the top and a quarter of the way in from the sides. This helps move the eye around the quilt. You can center it around one of your blocks or you can start dead center; it's entirely up to you.

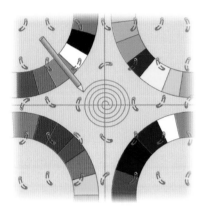

1 Prepare your "quilt sandwich" as described on page 18. Start by using a scrap piece of fabric to determine the distance between the stitch and the side of your walking foot. You can increase the width by adjusting the needle position to either the left or the right of center in your foot. Once you have a dimension, draw a simple spiral shape on your quilt top with a quilter's pencil, leaving a consistent gap between the concentric lines of the spiral.

2 Once you start stitching, place the edge of the walking foot along the previous row of stitches and use that as a guide, so that all your lines are the same distance apart.

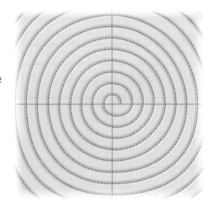

Straight lines

Draw out lines 2in (5cm) apart with a quilter's pencil or use painter's (masking) tape as a guide and stitch along the edge of the tape. The denser the quilting, the heavier the quilt will become due to the amount of thread added. I like to use the layout of the blocks or design as my starting point. If the quilt is mostly triangles, as here, I would choose one triangle and use the sides as my starting point.

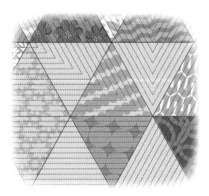

Grid or diamond quilting

When all else fails, a simple grid quilting of either square or diamond shapes is a great way to fill the space and not have the stitching be a focus of the quilt. You can make the grid quite wide or extremely tight. When working a long, straight line that doesn't have a seam to use for reference, use a long length of painter's (masking) tape as a guide. The low-tack tape is perfect, because it will not leave any glue on your quilt top. I like to use the tape along with the side of the foot when quilting this way. Some people like to stitch along the edge of the tape; but if you waver slightly, you will need to pull the tape out from between the stitches.

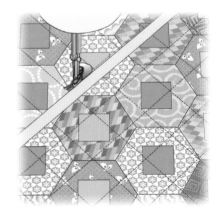

Binding

Binding adds the last little signature to your quilt that states your style. Some people only use solid fabrics for their binding; others use a coordinating print that matches the top. Then there is me (and I am sure others); I like to use scraps and multiple prints when making binding. Whichever category you fall into, this is the way to make perfect binding.

Making binding strips

1 I prefer to cut my binding into 2½-in (6.5-cm) strips. Depending on the size of your quilt you may need several strips—to figure out the amount you will need, you can find binding calculators online or simply double the length and width, add them together, and then add 20in (51cm). So if your quilt is 45 x 60in (114.25 x 152cm), you will need to cut 45 x 2 = 90, 60 x 2 = 120, 90 + 120 + 20 = 230in (584cm).

2 You now need to divide the length of binding needed by the width of the fabric (WOF), which is usually 44in (112cm)—but you don't want to use the selvage, so divide 230 by 42 = 5.5 strips. So cut six 2½-in (6.5-cm) x WOF strips to complete the binding.

3 Place one of your binding strips horizontally on the table in front of you, RS up. At the far right place the second strip, RS down vertically, overlapping the edges. This will create a 90-degree corner. Pin and then draw a single diagonal line from the upper left to the lower right; this will be your sewing line. With a slightly shorter stitch length, sew along the drawn line from point to point.

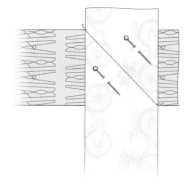

4 An alternate method uses a piece of painter's (masking) tape and will eliminate the drawing of the lines. Using your quilter's ruler, line up the edge of the ruler with the needle and place the tape along the ruler's edge on your machine base.

5 Position and pin your fabric as you did in step 3. With your needle in the down position, place it at the corner where the fabric crosses. Align the second corner with the edge of the tape. Slowly stitch between these two points, making sure to keep the end corner aligned with the tape.

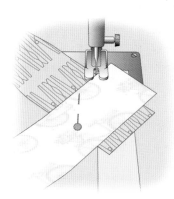

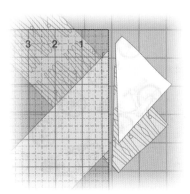

6 When all of your WOF strips have been stitched on the miter, you can now trim away the extra fabrics. Place your ruler's ¼-in (6-mm) line along the stitches and cut. Do this to all of the seams.

7 Open the fabric and then press the seams open. This will help spread the bulk in the bound edge. Then, starting at one end, use a hot iron and stem to press the binding in half lengthways, with WS together. If I am not planning on attaching it at that moment, I like to roll my binding around my hand for easy storage.

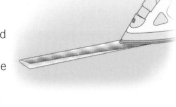

Squaring your quilt

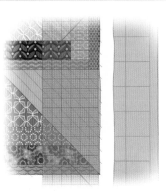

1 Place your finished quilt sandwich on your cutting surface, and use a long quilter's ruler to align the edge to be trimmed. Use the ruler's markings to help keep the edge straight. Cut off the excess fabric with a rotary cutter.

2 Stop before you reach the end of the ruler and reposition your quilt on the cutting mat. With your cutter in position where you left off, align the ruler again and continue working your way to the end of the first side.

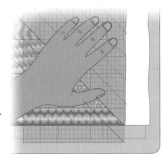

3 When you have cut the first side, rotate the quilt. Again using your ruler, line up the markings on the previously cut edge to make sure the next edge will be square to the first one. Cut along the untrimmed side. Repeat on all four sides.

Adding hanging corners

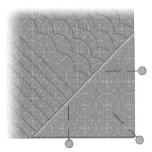

1 Cut two pieces of fabric at least 5in (12.5cm) square from your leftover backing fabric—or use a contrast fabric. Using a hot iron, press each square in half diagonally with WS together. On the back of your quilt, before you attach your binding, align the raw edges of a triangle on each of the two top corners and pin in place.

2 Adjust your needle position so you are stitching about ⅛in (3mm) in from the outer edge of the triangle. Start by backstitching, then stitch to the corner and stop with the needle in the down position about ⅛in (3mm) from the end. Rotate the quilt to align the next edge and continue stitching. Backstitch at the end to lock the threads. Repeat on the other quilt corner and then move on to binding your quilt.

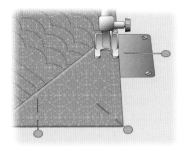

TIP

You never know when your masterpiece will need to be hung on a wall. Adding simple hanging corners before binding allows you the flexibility to do this, without taking away from the quilt. You can use leftover backing fabric so the hanging corners will blend in, or make them in a contrasting fabric to add a punch of color.

Attaching the binding

1 First test your needle position with a small offcut from your squared up quilt and a 3–4-in (7.5–10-cm) strip of your binding. I like my 2½in (6.5cm) binding to have about a ⅜in (1cm) face—the width that shows on the RS. Place the raw edges of the folded binding along the cut edge of the quilt sandwich and stitch with a ⅜-in (1-cm) seam allowance, using a 2 to 2.5 stitch length. Break the thread and then fold over the binding to make sure your positioning is correct.

2 Once you are satisfied with your test, place the longest side of your quilt under your presser foot, with the quilt top face up and the needle about 12in (30.5cm) from the bottom corner. Place your binding edge so it begins at the middle of the long edge. You will begin your stitching 12in (30.5cm) from the end and so have an unsewn tail of binding toward the top, which will be used for joining the binding ends later.

3 Backstitch at the beginning, then using a ⅜-in (1-cm) seam allowance, slowly stitch the binding to the quilt, stopping about ⅜in (1cm) from the bottom corner. Placing a pin ⅜in (1cm) in and ⅜in (1cm) up from the bottom will help you locate your point. Use your hand wheel for more control and stop with the needle down. Lift the presser foot and swivel the quilt and binding 45-degrees clockwise to face the corner. Sew off the corner—this will help to create the mitered corner.

4 To create the crisp mitered corner, remove the quilt from the machine. With the sewn binding in the vertical position, take the unsewn binding and fold it back along that 45-degree stitching line and then finger press the diagonal fold.

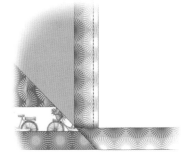

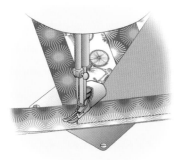

5 Using your finger to hold the corner in place, fold the binding back over itself to align the raw edge along the bottom of the quilt. This new fold should align with the outer edge of the sewn binding. Pin the new section down and prepare to sew again.

6 Work your way all around the quilt and stop about 24in (60cm) from your starting point, then backstitch. You will have a section that is unsewn where your binding will overlap. Find the center of the overlap and slide your quilter's ruler under both strips of binding. Mark the lower binding strip at the 2½-in (6.5-cm) mark on your quilter's ruler and the upper binding strip at the edge of the rule. Cut the excess binding away, leaving a 2½-in (6.5-cm) overlap of fabric.

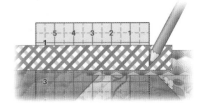

7 Open out the fold on the end of the left-hand binding strip and place it so it's RS up vertically in front of you. Open out the end of the right-hand side binding strip and align it RS down at a right angle to the left strip—as in Making Binding Strips, step 3. Align them perpendicular to each other. Draw a diagonal line from the upper left to the lower right across the corner, and then stitch along the line.

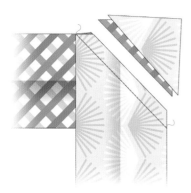

8 Trim off the excess to a ¼-in (6-mm) seam allowance through all layers.

9 Finger press (or use an iron if handy) the seam allowance open, then refold the binding in half. Reposition the binding back in place along the edge of the quilt. Start about ½in (12mm) behind the previous stitching, backstitch, and then continue to the starting point. Backstitch there as well, then cut the thread.

Hand sewing the binding

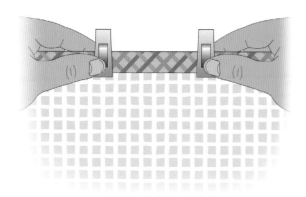

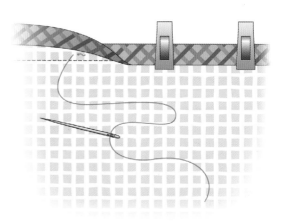

1 Once the binding is attached, you can start hand sewing the folded seam over to the back of the quilt. With the back of the quilt facing you, pull the binding firmly against the stitching line and fold it over to the back. Secure the binding with two hem clips (or any other clips) about 5–6in (12.5–15cm) apart.

2 Thread your needle with an 18–24-in (45–60-cm) length of thread and tie a knot in one end. To bury the knot in the quilt, insert the needle and thread under the folded binding close to the right clip, into the backing and batting layers.

3 Bring the thread out through the fold in the binding about ½in (12mm) from the insertion point. Begin hand stitching the fold down, taking 1/8–¼-in (3–6-mm) stitches down the edge of the quilt to the corner. Move and reposition the left clip as you reach it.

4 At the end of the first side, finish stitching about ½in (12mm) from the corner. Pinch the corner to create a 45-degree fold.

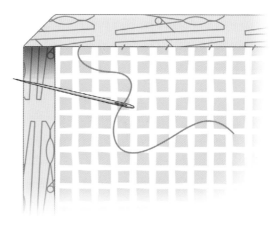

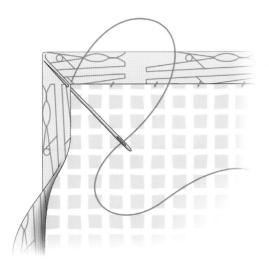

5 Pull the next length of binding over to the back, creating a neat mitered corner. Insert the needle into the quilt and exit at the bottom corner of the mitered binding. Pull the thread securely, and then take a stitch up the diagonal seam about half way to the point, bringing the needle out through the fold on top. Pull to secure and then make tiny stitches down the diagonal seam to close it.

6 Continue to stitch the binding in place, moving the clips along as you work, and working each corner in the same way. When you run out of thread, start a new length as described in step 2.

Hem tape binding

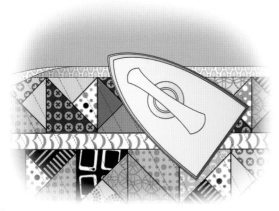

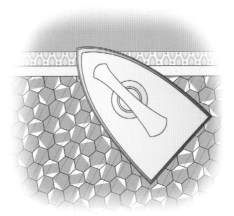

1 This alternative method avoids having to hand sew the binding down. First attach your binding to the front side of your quilt with your sewing machine as described on page 23. Working from the RS, use a hot dry iron to press the binding away from the quilt along the stitching line.

2 Flip your quilt over so the back is facing upward. Position a length of ¼in (6mm) wide double-sided hem tape glue side down as close to the edge of the quilt layers as possible. Fuse one side at a time to the quilt layers, using a hot iron. Work your way all around the quilt, folding a miter in the tape at the corners as you did on the front side before securing it in place with the iron.

3 Pull the protective paper off the hem tape and fold the binding up and over, making sure it covers the machine stitching used to attach the binding and the full width of the hem tape. Press the binding in place with a hot iron.

4 To finish, you can either topstitch along the folded seam from the RS or use one of your machine's decorative stitches. If you decide to use a decorative stitch, measure the width of the binding and run a test on scrap first, to make sure it will fit in the width of the binding.

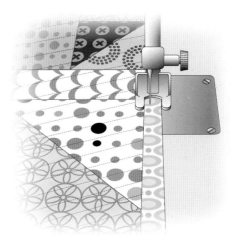

chapter 1
accessories and GIFTS

Everyone needs a little box or two (or seven) to keep little things from getting loose all over the house. These fun, simple no-piecing bins are a great place to keep your change when you empty your pocket—or make a big one to hold all your favorite quilting books. Plus, they can be stored flat when not in use.

Simple Fabric Boxes

For each box you will need

Fat quarter for the inside of the box

Fat quarter in a contrasting fabric for the outside

18 x 22in (46 x 56cm) of extra-thick double-sided fusible interfacing

White cotton thread for piecing and quilting

Basic kit (see page 8)

Double-sided tape

Finished size

Small box: 6 x 4¾ x 3¼in tall (15 x 12 x 8.25cm)

Medium box: 7 x 5½ x 3¾in tall (18 x 14 x 9.5cm)

Large box: 8 x 6½ x 4½in tall (20.25 x 16.5 x 11.5cm)

These boxes were made using fabrics from Maureen Cracknell's line from Art Gallery Fabrics called "Garden Dreamer." The interfacing used is Fast 2 Fuse medium weight. The threads used for stitching and quilting are from Aurifil.

Cutting

Press all fabric before cutting for easier piecing. If your fabric is not already cut into fat quarters, use the cutting list below for the size and quantity of each piece.

Inside fabric: Cut a fat quarter for each box

Outside fabric: Cut a fat quarter for each box

Interfacing: Cut a fat quarter for each box

1 Copy the template on page 118 onto cardstock as explained on page 15, enlarging it for the size of box you want to make. Join the parts as needed to make one piece.

2 Layer your fabrics by placing one print WS up, then the thick interfacing, followed by the second print fabric with RS facing up—just as you would if you were prepping your quilt sandwich. Follow the instructions from the interfacing and press all the layers together with a hot iron. Flip the "sandwich" over and press from the opposite side until the layers have fused completely.

3 With your ruler and rotary cutter, trim off any excess interfacing that may be sticking out—because it has a glued surface, it may stick to anything it comes into contact with. Removing it will eliminate any issues.

4 Bring your fused unit over to your machine and quilt like you would any other quilt. I like the look of random echo lines, so I started by making one sweeping line diagonally across the middle of the project. Then, using the width of my presser foot, I simply followed along the side and stitched parallel lines. I also adjusted my stitch length to a 4mm stitch for a more visible stitch.

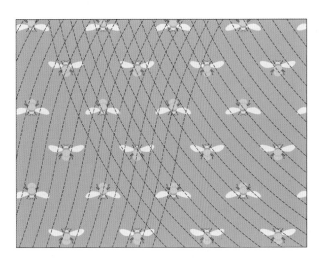

5 Position the cardstock template on the quilted fabric. To help keep it from moving around while trimming, place a few small pieces of removable double-sided tape on the reverse side of the template.

6 Using your ruler and rotary cutter, trim the outside edges of the template away. Continue trimming around the entire template. Switch to a smaller 18mm or 25mm rotary cutter to get into the tighter spaces.

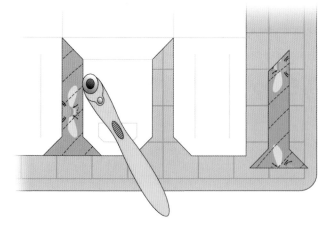

7 Adjust your stitch to a satin stitch of your choice—or even a fun decorative stitch would work, as long was you can manipulate the length. Position the long edge of the cut fabric box under your machine foot and begin stitching around the entire outside edge. You will need to stop and rotate the fabric at the corners; this is best done with your needle in the down position.

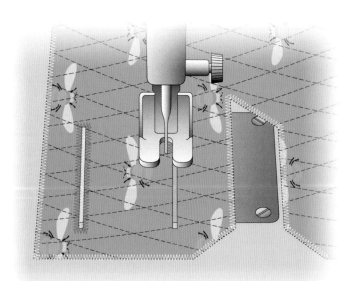

8 Once you have made it back to the starting point, backstitch a bit to lock in the threads. Reposition the fabric to stitch the slots. Repeat the same stitching on the eight slots.

9 Trim away any loose threads and your box is ready to be folded into shape. With the inside of the box face up in front of you, start by folding up each box side to crease the base square.

10 Then on one side overlap the two flaps with slots, aligning the slots. Take the handle flap and fold it over the two tucked-in sides, into the bottom slot, and then out through the upper slot. Repeat on the other side.

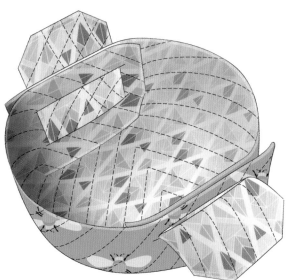

"First Love" Growth Chart

I have made a few of these growth charts as gifts for friends, and when our son was born, I made one for him. It's a simple 4-patch block spiced up with a few little tricks to a 9-patch, with a section for tracking your little one's height and date.

You will need

9 different print fabrics, each at least 8in (20cm) square—five dark and four light

⅓ yard (30.5cm) of fabric for sashing

⅓ yard (30.5cm) of white fabric

Fabric tape measure

55in (140cm) of ¼in (6mm) wide hem tape

17½ x 58½in (44.5 x 148.5cm) of batting (wadding)

17½ x 58½in (44.5 x 148.5cm) of backing fabric

⅓ yard (30.5cm) of binding fabric

White cotton thread for piecing and quilting

Basic kit (see page 8)

Finished size

11½ x 51½in (29 x 131cm)

This quilt was made using fabrics from Susan Emory's line from Michael Miller Fabrics called "Hank & Clementine." The batting (wadding) used is Warm and Natural supplied by The Warm Company. The threads used for piecing and quilting are from Aurifil. The tape measure is from East of India.

Cutting

Press all fabrics for the chart before cutting for easier piecing. Use the cutting list below for the size and quantity of each piece.

Print fabrics: cut four 3½-in (9-cm) squares from each print fabric

Sashing fabric: cut into 1½in (4cm) by WOF strips

White fabric: cut two 5 x 32-in (12.5 x 81-cm) strips

1 Each block consists of two darker print fabrics and a pair of light prints. Arrange them so the light fabrics are on opposite corners. Piece the two fabrics in each row together and press the seams in opposite directions. Nesting the seams in the center, pin and sew the rows together using a ¼-in (6-mm) seam allowance to create your basic 4-patch block.

TIP

Use a seam roller to quickly press your fabric without having to get up and iron.

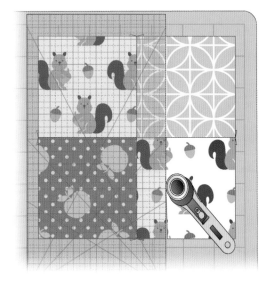

2 With your ruler, measure 1in (2.5cm) to the right of the center vertical seam and cut down the line. Measure 1in (2.5cm) to the left of the same center seam and cut down the line.

3 Rotate your block 90 degrees (having a rotating cutting mat here is a big help) and repeat the same cuts on either side of the seam. You will now have the pieces for a 9-patch block.

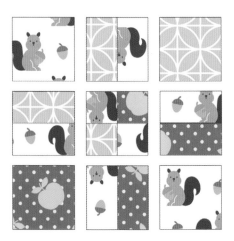

4 In row 1 you will be rotating the center block 180 degrees, in row 2 you will be rotating the center block and also switching blocks 1 and 3 (keep them in the same orientation), in row 3 you will rotate the center block 180 degrees as in row 1.

5 Piece together the three blocks in each row as you would with any 9-patch block, using a ¼-in (6-mm) seam allowance. Press the first and third rows to the left and the second row to the right. Sew the three rows together with a ¼-in (6-mm) seam allowance and press the seams flat. Repeat the process to complete a total of nine blocks.

6 Now add sashing on the bottom of all the blocks and also along the top of the first block. Place the sashing fabric in your machine and chain-piece (see page 17) the blocks to the sashing with a ¼-in (6-mm) seam allowance.

7 Cut the threads between the blocks, trim any excess sashing level with the blocks, and press them flat. Now you can sew the blocks together into one long strip with a ¼-in (6-mm) seam allowance, before adding long vertical sashing to both sides of the strip.

8 Using a ¼-in (6-mm) seam allowance, join the two pieces of white fabric into one long strip. Attach this to the right-hand side of the 9-patch strip and then add another 1½in (4cm) sashing strip to the right-hand edge of the white fabric.

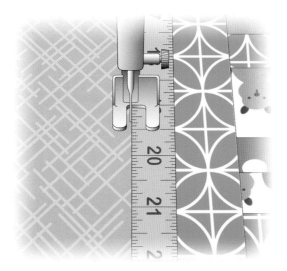

9 To add the fabric tape measure I used hem tape to temporarily glue it to the seam between the sashing and the white fabric. Set your machine to a decorative stitch of your choosing and sew down one long edge of the fabric tape. Once the first side is complete, turn and sew down the second side.

Backing, quilting, and binding

Spray-baste the quilt top to the batting and then to the backing fabric.

Use a quilter's pencil or a Henna Marker to draw horizontal lines at 1-in (2.5-cm) intervals. Stitch with your walking foot along the mark from once side to the other.

Prepare the binding and bind the edges of the quilt as described on pages 21–25.

English paper piecing (EPP) has been around for hundreds of years; the materials have changed, but the process of wrapping a display fabric around a piece of scrap fabric or paper has remained the same. The technique allows shapes to be connected easily by hand—no special tools are needed other than your hands, some fabric, paper or cardstock, and a needle and thread.

Hyde Park Pouch

You will need

Paper

6 fat quarter prints for outside of pouch

1 fat quarter print for lining

2 pieces of fusible interfacing, each 8 x 12in (20.25 x 30.5cm)

2 pieces of batting (wadding), each 8 x 12in (20.25 x 30.5cm)

1 zipper, 10in (25.5cm) long

White cotton thread for piecing and quilting

Basic kit (see page 8)

Hem clip

Finished size

6 x 10in (15 x 25.5cm)

This pouch was made using fat quarters from Dashwood Studios called "Street Life." The batting (wadding) used is Warm and Natural, supplied by The Warm Company. The threads used for piecing and quilting are from Aurifil.

Cutting

Press all fabrics for the pouch before cutting for easier piecing. Use the cutting list below for the size and quantity of each piece. Copy the template on page 123 onto a piece of cardstock as explained on page 15, enlarging it for the size of pouch you want to make.

Paper: Cut 50 hexagon shapes using the hexagon template

Motif prints: Fussy cut (see page 14) 24 motifs ¼in (6mm) larger all round than the hexagon template

Other prints: Cut strips ½in (12mm) wider than the hexagon template, center the template on the fabric, and cut out 26 pieces ¼in (6mm) larger all round than the template

Lining fabric: Cut two 6½ x 10¾in (16.5 x 27.25cm) rectangles

TIP

I printed and cut my hexagon shapes out of cardstock so that I can reuse them over again—my sizzix eclips 2 made quick work of cutting them.

1 With a hexagon fabric piece WS up, place your paper template on top and pin through the paper and fabric to secure the two together. To baste (tack) all of the templates, start by threading a needle and tie a quilter's knot at the end of the long thread.

2 Fold one long side of the fabric over the paper template and place a hem clip to hold it down. Now fold over a second edge, creating a folded corner. This is where you will insert your needle, taking a small bite of fabric. I like to stitch from the top folded fabric to the previous layer. Pull through to the knot to secure the first stitch. Take care not to stitch through the paper, as it will need to be removed at a later stage.

3 Fold over and create a tight corner on the next side, before inserting the needle through the two fabric layers in the same way. Secure the corner and repeat the process to turn the fabric over around the entire hexagon. Create two piles of 25 fabric-wrapped templates, one for each side of the pouch.

4 Take the first set of 25 and arrange them in three rows of eight, nine, and eight hexagons respectively.

5 Starting with the two left units in the center row, place them side by side as they will appear in the final project. Fold them together so the RS are facing and clamp them with a hem clip while you prepare your needle and thread.

6 Secure the long end of your thread with a knot and insert it approx. ¼in (6mm) from the edge to be joined to lock it in place. When joining EPP units, you want to insert and stitch through the fold of the fabric only. Sew inside the fold on one side and when the needle comes through the fabric, move directly below to the other fabric and insert the needle. Take a stitch about 1/16–1/8 in (1.5–3mm) long and repeat on the opposite side, working your way down the edge.

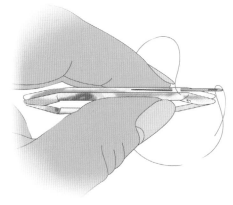

7 Every three to four stitches, give the thread a tug to pull the fabrics as close as possible. Finish with a slip knot. Repeat on all nine shapes so the center row is joined together into a strip.

8 Join the next row to the center row by aligning the top right block between the last two hexagons on the center row. Fold it down so a pair of short sides are matched and stitch this one seam with ladder stitch as before.

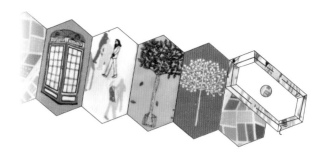

9 Repeat to add the first hexagon in the bottom row in the same way. Continue adding at the top and bottom, attaching each shape to the center row along one side only.

10 Now you are ready to attach the second short side of the top and bottom rows, but first carefully remove the paper from each center unit so it can be folded in half vertically. Align the open edge of each top and bottom shape in turn, and sew as you did before.

11 When all of the hexagons are attached and all of the paper templates have been removed, give the fabric a good press with your iron. Once flat and smooth, add a thin layer of fusible interfacing to the WS to give a bit more strength. Fuse the two together following the manufacturer's instructions.

12 Square up your fused fabric by cutting off half the end hexagon at each end of the center row and the points of the top and bottom row, so you have a 6½ x 10¾-in (16.5 x 27.25-cm) rectangle. Repeat steps 4 to 12 to create the second side of the pouch.

Quilting and making up

1 Place each rectangle of paper-pieced fabric on a layer of batting (wadding) and quilt as you desire—I quilted using a diamond pattern, using the width of my walking foot as the spacing.

2 To create your pouch, place one lining fabric piece RS up, with the zipper also RS up on top and aligned along the top edge. Add one of your quilted outer pieces RS down on top, aligning its top edge along the zipper and lining fabric edge. Pin in several spots along that edge.

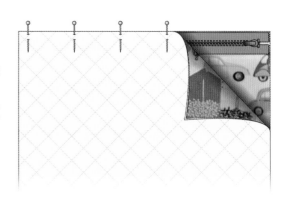

3 Sew with your zipper foot as close to the zipper teeth as possible. When you reach the zipper pull, pause with your needle in the fabric and the presser foot up. Reach under and pull the zipper pull to the sewn side. Continue stitching to the end.

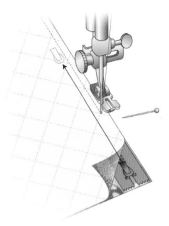

4 Open out and press the fabrics with WS together. Topstitch along the zipper to secure the layers in place.

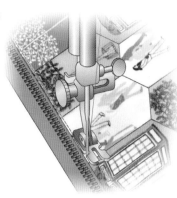

5 To attach the second side, place your second lining fabric RS up. Add the stitched piece with the zipper on top, with the two lining pieces RS together and the unstitched edge of the zipper aligned along the top edge. Place your second quilted outer piece RS down on top, with the top edge along the zipper and lining edge. Pin and sew as for the first side.

6 Open out the second side and press both sides flat so the lining and fronts are each WS together. Topstitch along the zipper on the second side to secure the layers in place.

7 Open your zipper wide enough so you can pull the pouch RS out later. Place the opened pouch on a table in front of you. Grab both of the quilted fronts and lift up RS together. While lifted, align all the edges of the lining fabric hanging below. Pin around all sides, leaving a hand-width opening between pins on the lining layers and making sure the zipper tape is pressed to the lining side.

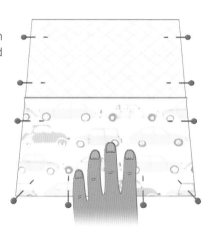

8 Starting at the pin on one side of the lining opening, backstitch and then sew all the way around the pouch with a ½-in (12-mm) seam allowance, taking care when you sew over the zipper sections. Stop sewing when you reach the second pin marking the lining opening and backstitch again.

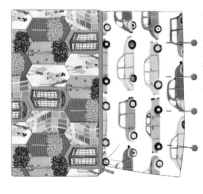

9 Clip the four corners to help remove excess bulk. Reach inside the pouch through the opening in the lining and pull the entire pouch RS out. Press under the edges of the opening by ½in (12mm) and topstitch it closed near to the edge.

10 Stuff the lining back inside the finished pouch.

Retreat Bag

Just like the "I Get Around" ironing mat (see page 49), for sewing gatherings you will also need to bring your supplies. For smaller local meet-ups I like to have my fabrics pre-cut, so I don't have to bring everything I own! This simple bag is the perfect size for your rulers, a small cutting mat, and your basic supply kit.

You will need

Twelve 5-in (12.5-cm) squares from a charm pack or cut from stash fabric

½ yard (0.45m) of strap fabric

½ yard (0.45m) of outer bag fabric

20 x 30in (51 x 76cm) of batting (wadding)

½ yard (0.45m) lining fabric

White cotton thread for piecing and quilting

Basic kit (see page 8)

Magnetic clasp (if using)

Finished size

12½ x 12½ x 2½in (31.75 x 31.75 x 6.5cm)

This bag was made using fabrics from my ever-growing stash. The batting (wadding) used is Warm and Natural, supplied by The Warm Company. The threads used for piecing and quilting are from Aurifil.

Cutting

Press all fabrics for the bag before cutting for easier piecing. Use the cutting list below for the size and quantity of each piece.

Charm pack/stash fabric: cut twelve 5-in (12.5-cm) squares for outer bag pockets

Strap fabric: cut into 4-in (10-cm) strips

Outer bag fabric: cut two pieces 13 x 14in (33 x 35.5cm), two pieces 3 x 14in (7.5 x 35.5cm), and one piece 3 x 13in (7.5 x 33cm)

Batting: cut two pieces 13 x 14in (33 x 35.5cm), two pieces 3 x 14in (7.5 x 35.5cm), and one piece 3 x 13in (7.5 x 33cm)

Lining fabric: cut two pieces 14 x 9½in (35.5 x 24cm), two pieces 13 x 14in (33 x 35.5cm), two pieces 3 x 14in (7.5 x 35.5cm), and one piece 3 x 13in (7.5 x 33cm)

TIP

To speed up the cutting process, simply stack your fat quarters along the selvage edge and cut as a unit. I like to cut four fabrics at a time. Any more than that and the fabric has a tendency to shift.

1 For the outer pockets on each side of the bag, arrange the 5-in (12.5-cm) squares into rows of three. Each side of the bag will need two rows, six fabrics per side. Stitch the three prints together in each row with a ¼-in (6-mm) seam allowance, press the seams to one side, then join the two rows, remembering to "nest" the matching seams (see page 17). Set aside.

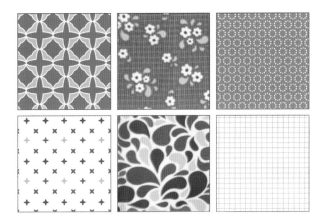

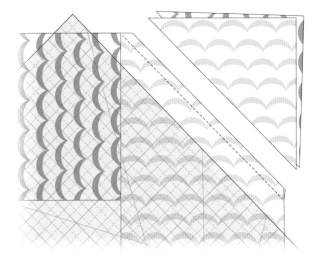

2 To create the shoulder straps, join the 4-in (10-cm) strips with a ¼-in (6-mm) seam allowance to the length of strap you want. I made a diagonal seam as a stronger join, and wanted my shoulder straps and bag to hang a bit lower, so I made the overall length of each strap around 48in (122cm).

3 Fold each shoulder strap in half lengthwise, WS together, and press to create a center crease. Open out flat and then fold each long edge to the center crease, pressing as you go. Refold along the center crease and press flat, so the long raw edges are now hidden inside. Topstitch along both sides of the strap.

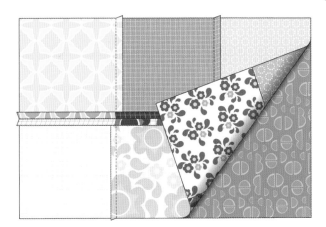

4 To create the inside lining for the outer pockets, place a pieced pocket RS together on one of the 14 x 9½-in (35.5 x 24-cm) lining pieces. Sew across the top edge with a ¼in (6mm) seam allowance. Press the seam open and fold so the WS are now together, then topstitch along the top edge. Repeat with the second set for the back.

5 The main bag sections will need to be quilted before final assembly to add a bit more stability to the overall bag. Take two 13 x 14-in (33 x 35.5-cm) main body pieces, two 3 x 14-in (7.5 x 35.5-cm) sides, and one 3 x 13-in (7.5 x 33-cm) bottom piece and place them WS down on top of the corresponding batting pieces. I quilted each section with simple parallel wavy lines. Choose a stitch you like and stitch the bottom and sides all over, but only the top 5–6in (12.5–15cm) of the body sections.

6 Place one quilted main body section RS up on your table. Add one of your outer pockets, aligning it at the bottom of the bag, and pin in place. Take one long strap and place one end centered over the pocket seam to one side of the center squares, with the raw edge at the bottom. Pin in a few places and then create the loop and align the other end to match on the other side of the center squares. Place the two top pins about 1½in (4cm) from the top of the bag—this is where you will stop topstitching before you turn and head back down.

7 Topstitch the strap in place along both side edges and across the top at the pin marker, then repeat steps 6 and 7 for the back of the bag.

8 Add the side strips on either side of the front section. Pin and sew using a ⅜-in (1-cm) seam allowance. Add the bottom strip to the back section in the same way. Press both pieces flat with a hot iron, with no steam.

9 Place the back/bottom section RS together with the front/sides section, centering the edge of the bottom piece along the bottom edge of the front. The ⅜-in (1-cm) seam allowance at each end of the bottom will extend over the two sides, so place a pin at the side seams as a guide for sewing. Stitch between the pins with a ⅜-in (1-cm) seam allowance, backstitching at the first pin and the end pin.

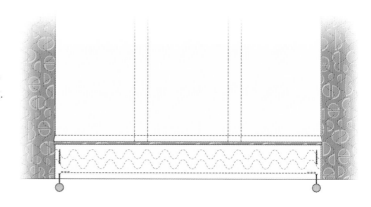

10 Fold to align the edge of one side panel to the back panel with RS together and pin to hold it in place. Sew together, stopping at the bottom and backstitching at the start and end of the seam. Repeat with the second side.

11 Fold, pin, and sew the bottom piece to the sides in the same way, creating the bottom boxed seam. Turn the outer bag RS out.

12 To create the inside lining, repeat steps 8 to 11 with the lining fabric pieces but leave the lining WS out at the end of step 11.

13 If you want to add a magnetic snap to close your bag, fix each half at the center and about 1in (2.5cm) below the top raw edge of the lining front and back pieces.

14 Insert the lining inside the outer bag with WS together and turn down the top edges of both sections. Press and pin the folded edges of bag and lining together. Be sure to tuck your straps out of the way (I stuffed them inside the pockets so they wouldn't get stitched) and then topstitch around the entire opening, joining the lining to the bag—I stitched a double topstitch for strength.

Everywhere you go, you will see adult coloring books. We even have a few of them in our house, but by far the biggest fan is my sister—I think I have counted around 15 books in her collection. Most of the time the pencils are all over the place and you can never find a pencil sharpener, so here's something cool to keep them all in one spot!

Coloring Book Holder

You will need

24 scraps of fabric to match colors of pencils

2 yards (1.85m) of denim fabric

¾ yard (65cm) of medium-weight fusible interfacing

½ yard (0.45m) of binding fabric

White cotton thread for piecing and quilting

Basic kit (see page 8)

Finished size

13¼ x 32¾in (33.5 x 83cm)

This holder was made using fabrics from my stash. The interfacing and denim were purchased from my local fabric supplier. The threads used for piecing and quilting are from Aurifil.

Cutting

Press all fabric for the holder before cutting for easier piecing. Use the cutting list below for the size and quantity of each piece.

Scrap fabrics: cut into 6½ x 1¼-in (16.5 x 3.25-cm) strips

Denim: cut four 2½ x 6½-in (6.5 x 16.5-cm) rectangles, three 2½ x 13-in (6.5 x 33-cm) rectangles, four 4 x 13-in (10 x 33-cm) rectangles, two 10 x 13-in (25.5 x 33-cm) rectangles, one 13 x 6-in (33 x 15-cm) rectangle, one 13-in (33-cm) square and one 29 x 13-in (73.5 x 33-cm) rectangle

Interfacing: cut two 12¾-in (32.5-cm) squares and one 9 x 12¾-in (23 x 32.5-cm) rectangle

TIP

Whenever possible, cut your fabrics for this project on the bias. It will give enough stretch for easy access to the pencil and supplies.

I like to cut denim with a sharp pinking blade on my rotary cutter—it will help keep the fraying down.

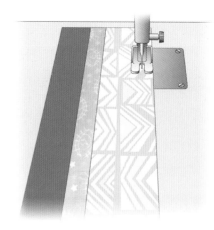

1 Lay out the 24 coloring pencils in front of you and then coordinate the colors to match. Split the pencils into two 12-pencil groups and sort out matching color scrap fabric strips. Piece the strips in the same order, using a ¼-in (6-mm) seam allowance, to make two striped panels each 6½in (16.5cm) tall and 12¼in (32.5cm) wide.

2 Add a 2½ x 6½-in (6.5 x 16.5-cm) piece of denim on each short side of both striped panels, using a ¼-in (6-mm) allowance. Once you have assembled the two striped panels, square up the bottom edge if needed and then cut each one down to 4½in (11.5cm) tall. Set aside the two 2-in (5-cm) strips you've cut off—you'll need them later.

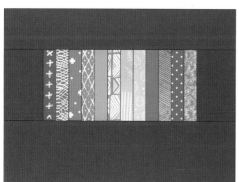

3 Next add a 2½ x 13-in (6.5 x 33-cm) piece of denim to the top and a 4 x 13-in (10 x 33-cm) piece to the bottom of both pieces, using a ¼-in (6-mm) allowance. Press the seam open and as flat as possible. Add an additional 2½ x 13-in (6.5 x 33-cm) strip of denim to the top edge of one piece only—the overall dimensions of this piece should now be 13in (33cm) square, so when folded over it will completely cover the book pocket.

4 For the pencil pockets, take the two 10 x 13-in (25.5 x 33-cm) pieces of denim and press both in half widthwise with WS together to create a piece measuring 5 x 13in (12.75 x 33cm). Make a double line of topstitching along each fold.

5 Place each topstitched pocket top over a striped pencil section and pin in place along the outer edges. Using your ruler and white marking pencil, draw stitching lines level with the seams of the striped panel to create the pencil pockets. Sew along each line.

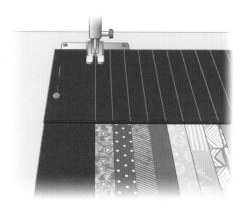

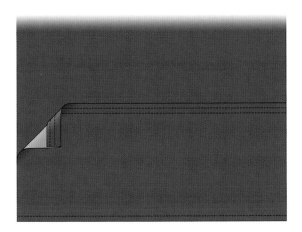

6 To create the pocket for the coloring book, take the 13 x 6-in (33 x 15-cm) piece of denim, fold over ¾in (18mm) along one long side, then make a double line of topstitching along the fold. Align the long raw edge of the pocket with the bottom of the 13-in (33-cm) square piece of denim, both with RS facing up, and sew with a ⅛-in (3-mm) seam allowance just to hold it in place—the binding will secure it properly at a later point.

7 The three main sections for the inside of the holder are now ready to be assembled. Place the book pocket square in the center with a pencil pocket on either side— the opening of both pencil pockets should be toward the center and the larger section for the front should be on the left side. With RS together, join the pieces with a ¼-in (6-mm) seam allowance and press the seams open. From the RS, topstitch along both sides of the seams for strength and looks.

8 For the outside cover, take the 29 x 13-in (73.5 x 33-cm) piece of denim and add one of the 2 x 13-in (5 x 33-cm) strips of striped fabric cut off in step 2 to each short end. Then add an additional 4 x 13-in (10 x 33-cm) piece of denim to each short end. Topstitch all of the seams.

9 Center the 9 x 12¾-in (23 x 32.5-cm) rectangle of fusible interfacing on the WS of the pocketed section. Add a 12¾-in (32.5-cm) square of fusible interfacing centered on each side. Then center the outside cover over the interfacing with WS together and, following the manufacturer's instructions, fuse all the layers together.

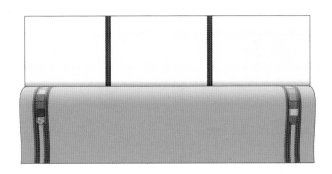

10 Using a decorative stitch, sew a few lines down on either side of the book pocket section to secure the layers and as a guide for where the folds are meant to be.

Binding

Prepare the binding and bind the edges of the coloring book holder as described on pages 21–25.

When you have kids, you always need to have floor pillows around the house. Making these fun floor pillows is a way to ensure that your sofa pillows remain on the sofa! I used a fussy cut large-scale print as the end of the "Zoom" and smaller prints for the sides and background.

Seventies Zoom Floor Pillow

You will need

Fat eighth of large-scale print yellow fabric

Fat quarter of medium-scale print medium blue fabric

Fat eighth of small-scale print light blue fabric

1 yard (1m) of solid light blue fabric for the bottom panel and boxing

22 x 22in (56 x 56cm) of batting (wadding)

20 x 20 x 3in deep (51 x 51 x 7.5cm) of memory foam (or regular foam pillow)

2 pieces of thick poly batting (wadding) larger than the foam

15–18in (38–46cm) long zipper

White cotton thread for piecing and quilting

Basic kit (see page 8)

Seam roller (optional)

Finished size

20 x 20 x 3in tall (51 x 51 x 7.5cm)

This quilt was made using fabrics from my stash. Memory foam was used for the pillow. The threads used for piecing and quilting are from Aurifil.

Cutting

Press all fabrics for the pillow before cutting for easier piecing. Use the cutting list below for the size and quantity of each piece. See page 10 for how to cut accurate squares, and page 14 for how to fussy cut.

Yellow: Fussy cut four 5-in (12.5-cm) squares

Medium blue: Cut four 5-in (12.5-cm) squares

Medium blue: Cut four 6-in (15-cm) squares

Light blue: Cut four 6-in (15-cm) squares

1 Make eight half-square triangles (HSTs) following the Double Method instructions on page 11, using the 6-in (15-cm) medium and light blue squares with RS together. Pin if you wish, and then sew ½in (12mm) away on each side of the drawn line. With your ruler and rotary cutter, align the edge of the ruler along the drawn line on the fabric and cut in half. Open out each square and press the seam toward the darker medium blue.

2 Once all the HST blocks have been assembled you will need to trim them to the final 5in (12.5cm) dimensions. Using your quilter's ruler with a 45-degree marking line, position the marking along the seam on the block and adjust so the square corner of the ruler is near the upper right corner.

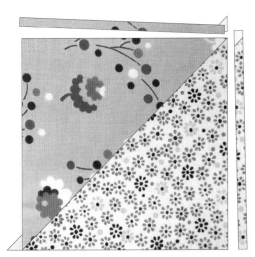

3 Trim the right-hand edge and the top with your rotary cutter. Rotate the block and trim to the final 5in (12.5cm) size, aligning both the 45-degree mark and the 5in (12.5cm) marks on the ruler to ensure a perfectly square cut. Arrange the HST blocks and 5-in (12.5-cm) yellow and medium blue squares as per the layout diagram on page 46, either on your design wall or a table top.

4 When assembling the rows, I always take the far left block and stack it on top of the block to the right. Then pick up the first two blocks together and stack on the third, and so on. Generally I do this one row at a time, so as not to accidentally rotate the blocks before the row is joined.

5 Take the first two blocks and place them side by side to confirm the orientation is still correct. Fold the right-hand block over so the RS are facing, and pin. Carefully move the unit to your machine and sew with a ¼-in (6-mm) seam allowance.

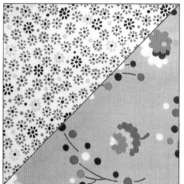

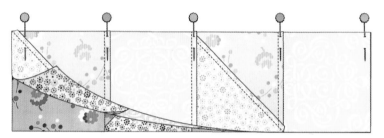

6 Repeat step 5 with the third and fourth blocks. Snip the thread tails and attach the 2-block units to finish the short row. Repeat the process with all the rows, following the layout diagram below left. You can now join the rows together. Place rows 1 and 2 face up in position, once again checking the orientation has not shifted. Flip the top row over onto the second row. Align the center seam and pin after "nesting" the meeting point (see page 17). Work your way to the left pinning all seams, and then to the right.

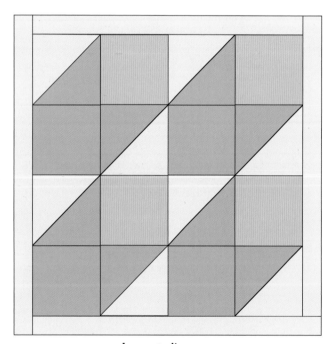

Layout diagram

7 Sew with a ¼-in (6-mm) seam, and then press the long horizontal seam open. Repeat with the remaining rows until you have a 18½-in (47-cm) square. By taking the time to carefully pin and sew a proper ¼-in (6-mm) seam, all of your points should match and align perfectly.

8 From the background light blue fabric, cut 2in (5cm) x WOF strips and add them to each side of the large block square so the finished size will be 21½in (54.5cm).

Backing and quilting

1 Place your quilt top on a piece of batting (wadding) a few in/cm wider on all sides. Make sure all the layers are nice and smooth, with no wrinkles. Baste (tack) the two layers together, using safety pins or your preferred method.

2 Quilt however you want to add a bit more strength and pillow to the overall project. I quilted in curved echo lines, using the width of my walking foot as spacers. Using your rotary cutter and quilter's ruler, square up the quilted top to 21½in (54.5cm) square.

Making up the pillow

1 Trim the memory foam to ½in (12mm) shorter on each side using a serrated knife, so it is 20½in (52cm) square. Cut the bottom fabric for your pillow to the same dimension as your top, so 21½in (54.5cm) square.

2 The memory foam measures 3in (7.5cm) tall. Add 1in (2.5cm) for the seam allowance and cut out 4-in (10-cm) strips long enough to go around three sides plus a few in/cm. Piece strips together if needed. This is called the boxing.

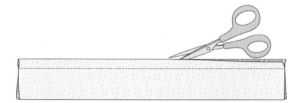

3 For the zipper boxing panel, measure the total width of the zipper. My zipper width was 1⅛in (3cm), so I added that to the boxing width of 4in (10cm) to get a panel that is 5⅛ x 19in (13 x 48.25cm). Cut the zipper boxing panel to this size. Press the zipper boxing panel in half, with RS together. Adjust your needle position to half the width of the zipper, so ⁹⁄₁₆in (15mm) from the right side of the presser foot. Sew down the folded edge, aligning the presser foot with the fold. With sharp scissors, cut along the fold the entire length of the panel and press the seam open.

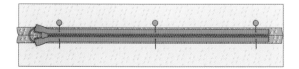

4 Place your zipper with the teeth face down on the WS of the zipper boxing panel. Center it along the seam and pin in place securely.

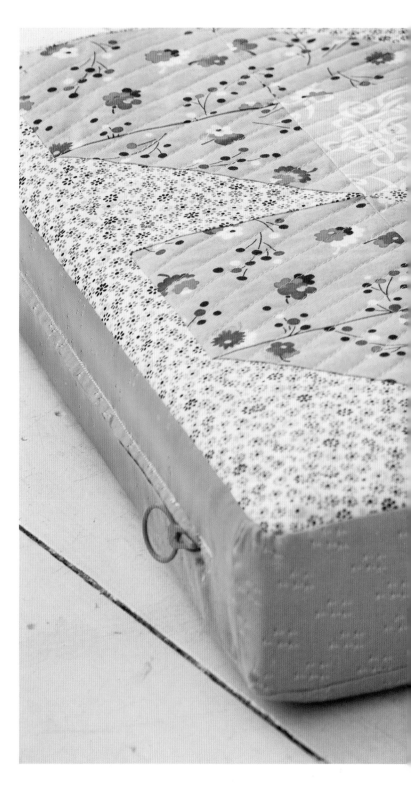

5 With your zipper foot attached to your machine, carefully sew the zipper in place all round. With your seam ripper, break the stitches over the zipper to reveal the pull. Open and close the zipper to make sure it works smoothly.

6 Your zipper boxing panel should now measure 4in (10cm) wide like the rest of the boxing. Attach one end of the zipper boxing panel to the side boxing with a ½-in (12-mm) seam allowance. Center the zipper panel section on the bottom of the quilted top. Pin along the edge, aligning as you work your way around the top.

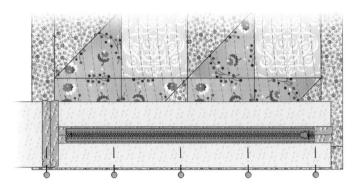

7 Attach the boxing all around the top with a ½-in (12-mm) seam allowance. Start in the middle of the zipper boxing panel and work your way to the corner, removing the pins as you come to them. Stop about 1½in (4cm) from the corner and prepare to slowly stitch the small rounded corner. You may want to snip into the boxing seam allowance to help with the stretch around the turn.

8 Continue working around the remaining sides until you reach the zipper boxing panel again. Measure and trim the excess boxing off and join it to the zipper panel. Finish stitching the boxing to the quilted top.

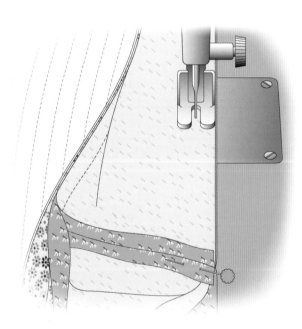

9 Repeat the marking and pinning to attach the other side of the boxing to the bottom panel. Stitch using the same ½-in (12-mm) seam allowance. Before stitching be sure to open the zipper about half to three-quarters of the way, so you will be able to reach in to turn the pillow RS out.

10 Clip across the corners off after the pillow has been assembled. This will help the corners come to a point. Before inserting the foam, cut and glue some poly padding to its top and bottom sides. Lay the foam on the padding, and cut along the sides with scissors. Using a spray glue for foam, spray the padding and the foam and press in place. This will help soften the edges of the pillow.

11 Fold the padded foam in half and insert it into the pillow cover. Some fiddling will be involved. Take your time and work the foam into the corners of the pillow. Zip the pillow closed and it is ready for use.

The "I Get Around" Ironing Mat and Sewing Machine Cover

With more and more sewing and quilting retreats taking place, I thought to make a handy travel ironing mat that can double as a cover for my machine when not in use (it's always in use). You can make it as is or simply add an old unfinished quilt top to the ironing surface and make a case/cover that fits your machine.

You will need

Fat eighth each of dark blue, orange dark plum, and red print fabric

Fat quarter each of teal, blue, lime, green, salmon, and plum print fabric

1 yard (1m) of white fabric

⅓ yard (30.5cm) of gray fabric

1½ yards (1.4m) of ironing surface fabric

1½ yards (1.4m) of batting/wadding (if ironing surface not already quilted)

24in (61cm) of canvas strap webbing

4 D-rings, 1in (2.5cm) wide, for the strap

4 metal grommets, 1½in (4cm) in diameter

4 heavy-duty magnetic snap sets

⅓ yard (30.5cm) of binding fabric

White cotton thread for piecing and quilting

Basic kit (see page 8)

Finished size

35½ x 46½ (90 x 118cm)

This quilt was made using fabrics from my stash. The ironing surface fabric was purchased from my local Joann Fabrics (it can be found online if your local shop doesn't have it). The threads used for piecing and quilting are from Aurifil.

Cutting

Press all fabrics for the cover before cutting for easier piecing. Use the cutting list below for the size and quantity of each piece.

Dark blue and orange fabrics: cut four 4½-in (11.5-cm) squares from each

Teal print fabric: cut two 4½-in (11.5-cm) squares and one 5 x 8¾-in (12.5 x 22.25-cm) rectangle

Blue print fabric: cut two 4½-in (11.5-cm) squares and one 5 x 8¾-in (12.5 x 22.25-cm) rectangle

Lime print fabric: cut two 4½-in (11.5-cm) squares and one 5 x 15¾-in (12.5 x 40-cm) rectangle

Green print fabric: cut two 4½-in (11.5-cm) squares and one 5 x 15¾-in (12.5 x 40-cm) rectangle

Salmon print fabric: cut two 4½-in (11.5-cm) squares and one 5 x 8¾-in (12.5 x 22.25-cm) rectangle

Plum print fabric: cut two 4½-in (11.5-cm) squares and one 5 x 15¾-in (12.5 x 40-cm) rectangle

Dark plum print fabric: cut one 5 x 8¾-in (12.5 x 22.25-cm) rectangle

Red print fabric: cut one 5 x 15¾-in (12.5 x 40-cm) rectangle

White fabric: cut four 5 x 8¾-in (12.5 x 22.25-cm) rectangles, four 5 x 15¾-in (12.5 x 40-cm) rectangles, four 5 x 4½-in (12.5 x 11.5-cm) rectangles, four 9¼ x 12-in (23.5 x 30.5-cm) rectangles, and one 2½-in (6.5-cm) square

Gray print fabric: cut two 2½ x 17¼-in (6.5 x 43.75-cm) lengths of sashing and two 2½ x 24-in (6.5 x 61-cm) lengths of sashing

1 I based the quilt top portion of this project on a barn quilt I found while driving around, and modified it to fit the dimensions of my machine. Start off by measuring the overall length of your machine, taking care to include the hand wheel. Then measure the depth at its deepest point and the full height from the table surface. Some machines will have external spool holders, which you will need to either remove or factor in.

2 Start with the 4½-in (11.5cm) squares for the four 4-patches at the center of the quilt. Making one block at a time, arrange your fabrics as per the photograph and piece them together using a ¼-in (6-mm) seam allowance. Press the two-unit rows in opposite directions for easier joining of the rows.

3 To create the Half Rectangle units, take a 5 x 8¾-in (12.5 x 22.25-cm) print fabric rectangle and a same size white rectangle. On the upper right and lower left short edge of each white rectangle, measure in and mark ¼in (6mm) from the sides. Draw a diagonal line between the points.

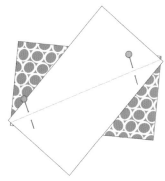

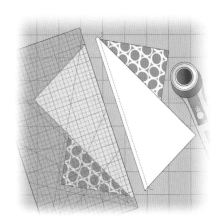

4 With the print rectangle RS up, measure in by the same ¼in (6mm) on the upper left and lower right short edge and put a mark. Using a pin to align the marked points, position the two rectangles RS together.

5 With your standard piecing foot adjusted to a ¼-in (6-mm) seam allowance, sew on both sides of the line drawn on the lighter fabric, as you would when making a standard HST block using the double method (see page 12). Cut your fabric along the drawn line and press the seam toward the darker color fabric to make two Half Rectangles. Repeat steps 3 to 5 to make four Half Rectangles. To make the four opposite direction rectangle units you will need to mark the opposite corners, but the sewing and cutting will remain the same.

6 Begin assembling the side sections by joining the Half Rectangle units and then attaching them to the 4-patch units, matching the photograph opposite for the layout.

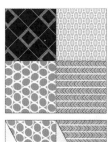

7 For the longer end sections, repeat steps 3 to 5 using the 5 x 15¾-in (12.5 x 40-cm) rectangles. Join the longer Half Rectangles in pairs, following the photograph.

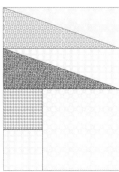

8 Using a ¼-in (6-mm) seam allowance, make up the four corners using the orange 4½-in (11.5-cm) squares and the remaining white rectangles. Join each corner to a longer Half Rectangle end section, following the photograph opposite, and then connect this to a side section to make up the four quarters of the quilt top.

9 When each of the four corner sections has been assembled, use a ¼in (6mm) seam allowance to add a 2½ x 17¼-in (6.5 x 43.75-cm) length of sashing to join the top two sections and then the two bottom sections.

10 Use the 2½-in (6.5-cm) white square to join the two longer lengths of sashing, and then use this to join the top and bottom halves, making sure the square is in the center. Press well to make sure all the seams are as flat as possible.

11 Quilt as desired—but instead of using backing material, use the ironing surface fabric. Some of these come already quilted on batting (wadding), but if you are using just the material without pre-sewn batting you will need to make up a quilt sandwich with your ironing surface fabric (RS facing down), the batting and the quilt top (RS facing up), as described on page 18.

12 After you have quilted your cover and trimmed it square to the final dimensions needed for your machine, you will need to measure in 5in (12.5cm) from both sides of each corner and put a pin. Place a quilter's ruler across the corner to connect the pins and cut off the corner with a rotary cutter.

13 Cut two 10-in (25.5-cm) lengths of webbing. Take two D-rings and insert them onto one end of one length of the webbing, then fold 2in (5cm) over to make a loop. Pin and sew the folded section of the webbing together, securing the rings in place. Repeat with the other length to make two straps with rings.

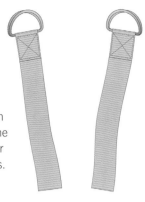

14 Divide the remaining length of webbing in half and seal the cut ends. These two pieces will be the opposite side of the D-rings.

15 Measure the space between the two hinged points of the sewing machine's handle and transfer this measurement to the two long sides on the back of the quilted cover. Pin a length of webbing at each point on one side, and a D-ring strap at each point on the other side, lining up the raw ends with the outer edge of the cover. The straps will need to go inside the handle, for the handle to still be usable. Stitch within the binding space to secure all the straps.

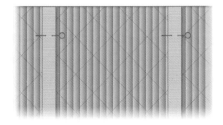

16 Attach the binding to your quilted mat cover as you would normally, following the instructions on pages 21–25. Carefully fold the angled corners.

17 The four grommets will be positioned on the clipped diagonal corners of the mat, about 1in (2.5cm) from the edge. Position each grommet as shown in the photograph on page 50 and mark the inner circle with a pencil. Using a sharp-pointed pair of scissors, cut the marked circles so the two-part grommets can be inserted and secured, following the instructions on the packet.

18 To find the correct positions for the magnetic clasps, place your machine on the ironing side of the mat, centering it as best you can.

19 Fold up both long sides of the mat and attach the straps through the D-rings to hold the sides up in place. Grab the top bound edge of one extended end of the mat directly above the end of the machine base and fold it back toward the machine. This will bring the short side up. Fold in each side to the "travel" position as shown in the photograph on page 49.

20 Using a pencil through the grommet, mark the inside and outside location for the two halves of the magnetic clasp. Center one half of the clasp over the mark and draw two cut lines for the prongs of the clasp mounts. Using a sharp small blade, cut the two slits and insert the prongs through the cuts. Place the cap and fold down the prongs to secure one side. Repeat on the opposite mark to complete the clasp set. Repeat at all four grommets.

Accent pillows don't always have to be square or rectangle.
They can look really comfy as a round boxed pillow, too!

Round Boxed Pillow

You will need

⅓ yard (30.5cm) of various scrap fabrics

20-in (51-cm) square of print fabric

20-in (51-cm) square of batting (wadding)

¼ yard (25cm) of boxing fabric

14-in (35.5-cm) zipper

18in (46cm) diameter circle of Home Foam, 3in (7.5cm) thick, or an 18-in (46-cm) circular pillow form (cushion pad)

Basic kit (see page 8)

Finished size

18in (46cm) in diameter

This quilt pillow was made using fabrics from Betsy Siber's range called "Everglades" from Michael Miller Fabrics. The batting (wadding) used is Warm and Natural and the 3in (7.5cm) home foam was supplied by The Warm Company. The threads used for piecing and quilting are from Aurifil.

Cutting

Press all fabrics for the pillow before cutting for easier piecing. Use the cutting list below for the size and quantity of each piece.

Scrap fabrics: cut into 2½ x 18-in (6.5 x 46-cm) strips

Print fabric: cut one 19-in (48.25-cm) circle

Boxing fabric: cut one 5 x 18-in (12.5 x 46-cm) strip and two 4in (10cm) wide strips

1 Follow the steps in the Downpour Quilt (see page 97) to make up a 20-in (51-cm) square of pieced fabric.

2 Take the square and fold it into quarters by matching diagonally opposite points on the square and then folding the resulting triangle in half again.

3 Because most compasses will not expand to create a 19-in (48.25-cm) circle, I made a template to mark the fabric on the WS. Place a pin at the folded point and use that as your center anchor to mark a sweeping arc with a pencil. Using a rotary cutter, cut along the drawn line and discard the scrap.

4 Unfold the circle and spray baste it to a layer of batting (wadding). Quilt the layers as you wish—I quilted a spiral radiating out from the center of the circle.

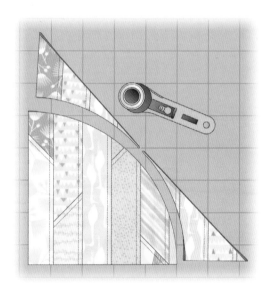

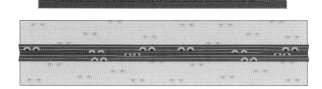

5 Fold the 5-in (12.5-cm) boxing fabric strip in half lengthwise, RS together, and press with a hot iron. Sew along ½in (12mm) from the folded edge—this width should be half the width of the zipper, which in my case was 1in (2.5cm). Cut along the fold with sharp scissors and press the seam open.

6 Center the zipper along the pressed-open seam and pin in place for stitching. With your zipper foot attached to your machine, carefully sew the zipper in place all round. Turn the piece over to the RS and use a seam ripper to open the seam over the zipper.

7 Join the 4-in (10-cm) wide boxing panel strips with a ¼-in (6-mm) seam allowance to make one strip approximately 50in (12cm) long. It will be a touch longer than you will need. Press the seams open.

8 With RS together, add your 4in (10cm) wide boxing strip to one end of the zipper panel with a ¼-in (6-mm) seam allowance, and press the seam open.

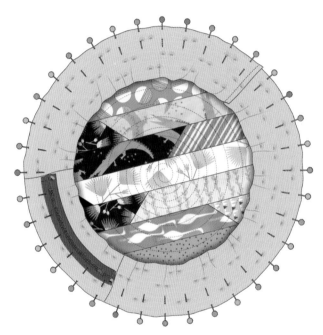

9 Beginning with the zipper panel, attach the boxing to the quilted pillow top by pinning every 2in (5cm), while easing the fabric around the circle. When you reach the other end of the zipper panel, join it to the end of the boxing strip with a ¼-in (6-mm) seam allowance and cut off any excess boxing.

10 Sew the boxing to the pillow top with a ½-in (12-mm) seam allowance, and then repeat the pinning process to add the print fabric circle for the back. Be sure to open the zipper before pinning and sewing on the back.

11 If you don't have access to an 18-in (46-cm) circle pillow form (cushion pad) you can easily make one by using a template to mark the circle to be cut on a square of foam. Because the foam is too thick to cut in one pass, take small shallow passes around the marking until it is completely cut.

12 Pull the stitched pillow cover RS out and insert the foam through the zipper opening by folding it in half. Close the zipper to finish.

chapter 2

blankets and QUILTS

Color Wheel Mini Quilt

We all have stash fabric in our collection that we just don't know what to do with. Why not take a few small bits from each piece and incorporate them into this fun mini quilt?

You will need

3 x 10in (7.5 x 25.5cm) each of 7 pink/red fabrics, ranging from dark to light

3 x 10in (7.5 x 25.5cm) each of 7 red/purple fabrics ranging from dark to light

3 x 10in (7.5 x 25.5cm) each of 7 purple/violet fabrics ranging from dark to light

3 x 10in (7.5 x 25.5cm) each of 7 violet/blue fabrics ranging from dark to light

3 x 10in (7.5 x 25.5cm) each of 7 blue/teal fabrics ranging from dark to light

3 x 10in (7.5 x 25.5cm) each of 7 teal/green fabrics ranging from dark to light

3 x 10in (7.5 x 25.5cm) each of 7 yellow fabrics ranging from dark to light

3 x 10in (7.5 x 25.5cm) each of 7 orange fabrics ranging from dark to light

Fat quarter of white fabric

Fat quarter of dark background fabric

2 x 18-in (46-cm) squares of batting (wadding)

Fat quarter of backing fabric

¼ yard (0.25m) of binding fabric

White cotton thread for piecing and quilting

Basic kit (see page 8)

Seam roller (optional)

Finished size

17 x 17in (43 x 43cm)

This quilt was made using fabrics from Art Gallery Fabrics new Color Masters Fat Quarters. The batting (wadding) used is Warm and Natural, supplied by The Warm Company. The threads used for piecing and quilting are from Aurifil.

Cutting

Press all fabrics for the quilt top before cutting for easier piecing. Use the cutting list below for the size and quantity of each piece.

Color fabrics: Cut one 3 x 10-in (7.5 x 25.5-cm) rectangle from each of the 56 prints

White fabric: Cut eight 3 x 10-in (7.5 x 25.5-cm) rectangles

1 Start by arranging your seven color fabrics for each of the eight sections from light to dark. The lightest will be fabric 1, through to the darkest as fabric 7. Scan and print out or photocopy four copies of Template A and four of Template B on page 125. The templates are numbered to show you which fabric goes where.

2 Begin with fabric 1, the lightest on your table, RS up. Place a rectangle of white fabric on top of fabric 1, RS together. It's not crucial, but try to center as best as you can. Position a template with the lines face up. Arrange it so the line between the segment marked "white" and the segment marked "1" on the template is close to the left side of the fabrics—that line will be our first stitched seam line. Pin through the paper and fabric to keep the layers from shifting.

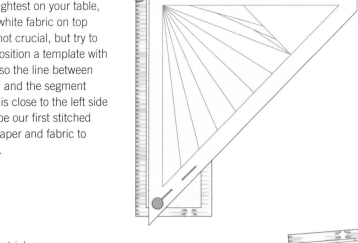

3 You may need to do some trial runs stitching through the paper. You want the stitches to be small enough that they tear away like a perforated paper, but not so small that they fall apart while sewing. You also don't want them so big that they don't tear away easily. I would suggest trying 1.2 as your stitch length and see how it goes. You can always adjust up or down as needed. Rotate your hand wheel so you are starting right on the point where the lines begin.

4 Stitch slowly along the line. Stop when you reach approx. ¼in (6mm) beyond the end of the marked line

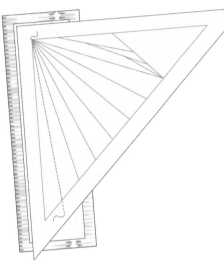

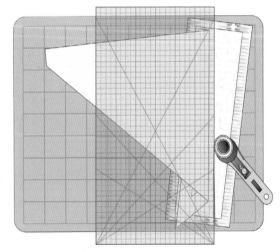

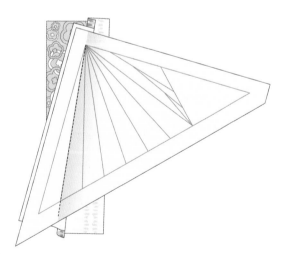

5 Fold the paper back along the stitched line so you can trim away the excess fabric in the seam allowance. Place the ruler along the fold aligned with the ¼-in (6-mm) mark. With your rotary cutter, trim away both layers of excess fabric and discard.

6 Press the template open again so you are ready for the next print fabric. Position fabric 2 on the table in front of you, RS up, and then place the template with its attached fabrics RS down on top. Align the left side of fabric 2 about ½in (12mm) away from the next line to be sewn, between segments 1 and 2.

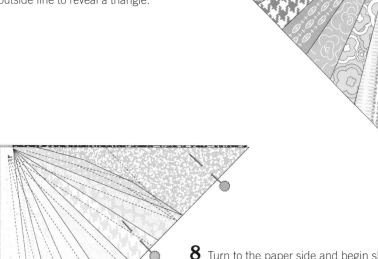

7 Repeat this process with all the print fabrics and also the background fabric. When the template has been fully pieced, trim away the excess fabric on the outside line to reveal a triangle.

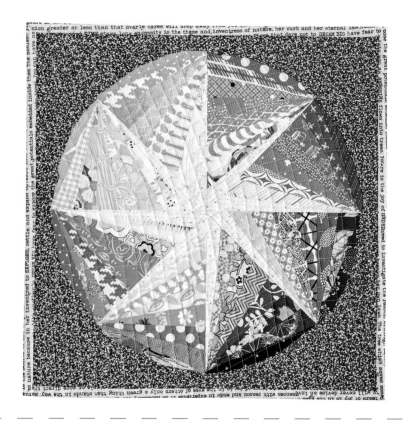

8 Turn to the paper side and begin slowly and carefully removing the paper from the fabric. The shapes should pull apart easily. When all the triangles have been pieced and cut, refer to the photograph below to pair up two triangles to make a corner square. With RS together, pin and then sew the long sides.

9 Repeat steps 2 to 8 to make the other three squares, then position the squares on your design wall (or floor). You can now piece together the square blocks in two rows, by placing the right block over the left and sewing with a ¼-in (6-mm) seam allowance. Press the seams open as best you can, then join the rows—there will be a bit of bulk in the points from the layers converging.

Backing, quilting, and binding

Make a quilt sandwich (see page 18) from your backing fabric (RS facing down), the batting (wadding), and the quilt top (RS facing up). I used two layers of batting to add a bit more cushion to the bulky areas. Make sure all the layers are nice and smooth, with no wrinkles. Baste (tack) all three layers together, using safety pins or your preferred method.

Quilt as you prefer—I decided to quilt this project using my walking foot and a grid of sweeping echo curves (see page 20).

Prepare the binding and bind the edges of the quilt as described on pages 21–25.v

Good Vibrations Quilt

Figuring out what to do with a jelly roll is always a challenge, but adding a bit of yardage to the mix opens up the possibilities. Use a denim or even a contrasting print fabric as the other half of the half-square triangle and you are off to explore the endless designs you can make. The fun pastel colors from the jelly roll had me thinking beach from the get go. I put some Beach Boys on the stereo and had a blast making this quilt. Nothing but "Good Vibrations"!

You will need

Jelly roll of pre-cut fabrics

1¼ yards (1.15m) of background fabric (denim)

Fat eighth of contrasting fabric

3 yards (2.75m) of backing fabric; I used two contrasting fabrics joined with a horizontal seam

52 x 73in (132 x 185.5cm) of batting (wadding)

½ yard (0.5m) of binding fabric

White cotton thread for piecing and quilting

Basic kit (see page 8)

Seam roller (optional)

Finished size

45½ x 67in (115.5 x 170cm)

This quilt was made using a jelly roll from Moda Fabrics that I have had lying around for ages—they look so nice all rolled up that I never want to open them. The batting (wadding) used is Warm and Natural, supplied by The Warm Company. The threads used for piecing and quilting are from Aurifil.

Cutting

Press all fabrics for the quilt top before cutting for easier piecing. Use the cutting list on the right for the size and quantity of each piece. See page 10 for how to cut accurate squares. Separate your jelly roll into two piles, one light and one dark—each block will use one strip of fabric from the light and one from the dark side. Pair up the fabrics that work well together if you choose, or simply pull at random.

Light fabric: Cut twelve 2½-in (6.5-cm) squares, twelve 2½ x 6½-in (6.5 x 16.5-cm) rectangles, twelve 1¼ x 10½-in (3.25 x 26.5-cm) strips, and twelve 1¼ x 12½-in (3.25 x 31.75-cm) strips

Dark fabric: Cut twelve 2½-in (6.5-cm) squares, twelve 2½ x 6½-in (6.5 x 16.5-cm) rectangles, twelve 1¼ x 10½-in (3.25 x 26.5-cm) strips, twelve 1¼ x 12½-in (3.25 x 31.75-cm) strips, and three 2-in (5-cm) squares

Denim fabric: Cut twelve 12-in (30.5-cm) squares and nine 2-in (5-cm) squares

1 Place your center square in front of you RS up and add one of your light squares next to it. Flip over the light fabric so it is now RS together and align the edge for piecing. Stitch with a ¼-in (6-mm) seam allowance. Repeat with the second light square on the opposite side of the center.

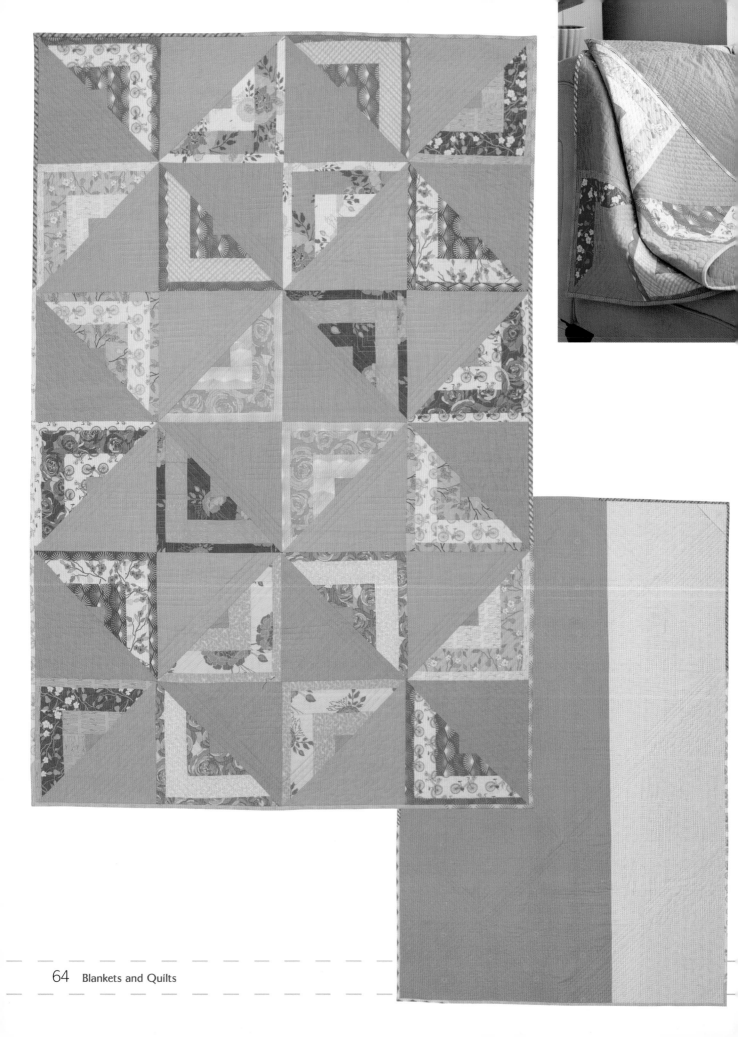

2 Press the seams and position the block back in front of you. Add the two side pieces to the center rectangle in the same fashion. Repeat the piecing process by adding 6½-in (16.5-cm) dark rectangles to the top and bottom of the block and then add 10½-in (26.5-cm) dark rectangles to the sides. Press after each seam. Add the outside frame to the block by attaching thin rectangles of light fabric to the top, bottom, and sides.

3 Repeat the process to end up with six framed blocks, then make another six framed blocks with the light and dark fabrics reversed.

4 My denim fabric has a slightly lighter side on the top and I wanted to use that slight difference, so I took six of the 12-in (30.5-cm) squares and drew a line diagonally across the reverse side and then drew a line diagonally on the top side of the remaining six.

5 Stack a marked denim square on top of the framed block, RS together. Pin as needed and carefully sew a ¼-in (6-mm) seam allowance on either side of the marked line. After stitching, use your ruler and rotary cutter to cut along the line.

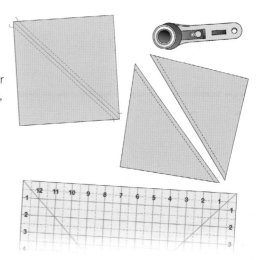

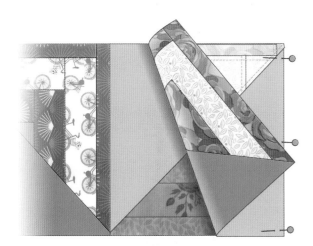

6 Repeat the process on all of the 12 blocks. Position on your design wall (or floor) arranging the blocks in a pinwheel design, following the photograph on page 64. Start by stitching the blocks together into rows, then stitch the rows into a completed quilt top.

Backing, quilting, and binding

Make a quilt sandwich (see page 18) from your backing fabric (RS facing down), the batting (wadding), and the quilt top (RS facing up). Make sure all the layers are nice and smooth, with no wrinkles. Baste (tack) all three layers together, using safety pins or your preferred method.

Quilt as you prefer—I decided to quilt this project using my walking foot, making square spirals and frames around the blocks. In other sections I adjusted the stitch to create fun scallops, and echoed them in adjacent sections.

Prepare the binding and bind the edges of the quilt as described on pages 21–25.

With a bunch of my friends having babies, I wanted to come up with a fun quilt that looks more complex than it is. Designing with simple double-half-square triangles can be a fun and quick way to achieve the "spent a lot of time"-looking quilt. So press, cut, and stitch your way through the universe with this Rocket Boy quilt.

Rocket Boy

You will need

1¼ yards (1.15cm) of black fabric

1¼ yards (1.15cm) of teal fabric

1¼ yards (1.15cm) of white glow-in-the-dark fabric

¾ yard (0.70m) of red fabric

¾ yard (0.70m) of light blue fabric

55 x 63in (140 x 160cm) of batting (wadding)

3½ yards (3.2m) of backing fabric

½ yard (0.45m) of binding fabric

White cotton thread for piecing and quilting

Basic kit (see page 8)

Seam roller (optional)

Finished size

49 x 57in (124.5 x 145cm)

This quilt was made using fabrics from Michael Miller Fabrics called "Rocket Kids". The batting (wadding) used is Warm and Natural, supplied by The Warm Company. The threads used for piecing and quilting are from Aurifil.

Cutting

Press all fabrics for the quilt top before cutting for easier piecing. Use the cutting list to the right for the size and quantity of each piece. See page 10 for how to cut accurate squares.

Black fabric: Cut fourteen 5½-in (14-cm) squares and seven 9½-in (24-cm) squares

Teal fabric: Cut fourteen 5½-in (14-cm) squares and seven 9½-in (24-cm) squares

White glow-in-the-dark fabric: Cut fourteen 5½-in (14-cm) squares and seven 9½-in (24-cm) squares

Red fabric: Cut seven 5½-in (14-cm) squares and four 9½-in (24-cm) squares

Light blue fabric: Cut seven 5½-in (14-cm) squares and four 9½-in (24-cm) squares

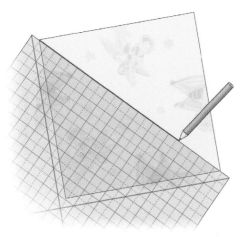

1 The process for completing each block will be the same. On the reverse side of your light blue and red fabrics draw a diagonal line with a pencil or a pen. You don't need to use a quilter's pen—a regular ballpoint is fine, as the line drawn will indicate the cutting line in a later step.

2 Place a white square RS up, with the same size of light blue or red fabric square WS down on top. Align the edges so all four sides match. Pin if you desire and bring to your machine. You should have a foot that will allow you to sew a scant ¼-in (5-mm) seam allowance. Adjust the needle position until you are happy with the placement.

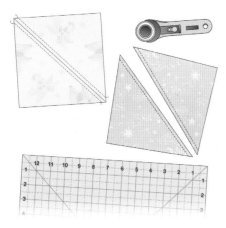

3 Begin sewing a ¼-in (5-mm) seam on the left side of the diagonal line drawn on the fabric. When you get to the end, you can either cut the thread and reposition, or simply raise the presser foot and rotate the fabric so the other side of the line can be sewn. With your ruler and rotary cutter, align the edge of the ruler along the drawn line on the fabric and cut each square in half.

4 Keeping the diagonal cut edges perfectly aligned, cut each HST unit in half from the point of the one triangle to the point of the other triangle.

5 Set the seams by pressing down with a hot iron. To help with aligning the centers, I recommend pressing your fabric to the darker side on both the light blue and red blocks, so open the triangles out and press the seam toward the darker fabric. Repeat steps 2 to 5 with the black and teal fabric squares.

6 Arrange pairs of triangles into new blocks, following the photograph opposite as a guide. Placing a pair of triangles RS together, nest the center seam (see page 17) by adjusting it between your thumb and index finger. Because the seams have been pressed toward the darker side, they should nest tightly together.

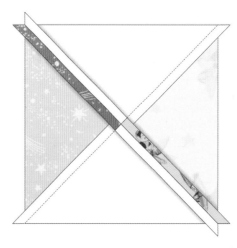

7 Pin and sew a ¼-in (6-mm) seam down the long edge. Press the new center seam open. This will help distribute the bulk evenly.

8 Trim all the smaller blocks to measure 4½in (11.5cm) square. Position the square corner of the ruler and the diagonal 45-degree marking along the center of the block, locating the half measure—2¼in (5.75cm).

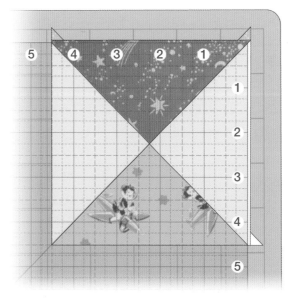

9 Trim away the excess fabric using your rotary cutter. Rotate your block 180 degrees and square up to 4½in (11.5cm). You can also double-check it's sized correctly by locating the center of the block and confirming it is at the 2¼-in (5.75-cm) mark on your ruler.

10 Repeat steps 1 to 9 to make 56 small blocks and 28 large blocks. Position the first line of small blocks vertically on your design wall/work surface according to the photograph above, and then pin and sew them together to make the first line of the quilt top.

11 Repeat to make three more rows of small blocks, and then make four rows of large blocks the same way. Join the vertical rows in order following the photograph to complete the quilt top.

Backing, quilting, and binding

Make a quilt sandwich (see page 18) from your backing fabric (RS facing down), the batting (wadding), and the quilt top (RS facing up). Make sure all the layers are nice and smooth, with no wrinkles. Baste (tack) all three layers together, using safety pins or your preferred method.

Quilt as you prefer—I decided to quilt this project with a series of lines radiating out from the center, and then added a line spiraling out from the center.

Prepare the binding and bind the edges of the quilt as described on pages 21–25.

Quilts don't always have to be a combination of dozens of different blocks. Sometimes an interesting block in two different colorways is all you need to have the wow factor. Easy to chain piece and quick as well.

Hypno Quilt

You will need

⅓ yard (30.5cm) of pink fabric

⅓ yard (30.5cm) of yellow fabric

⅓ yard (30.5cm) of green fabric

⅓ yard (30.5cm) of blue fabric

3 yards (2.75m) of light cream/white fabric

3 yards (2.75m) of dark gray/black fabric

79 x 82in (200 x 208cm) of batting (wadding)

4½ yards (4.2m) of backing fabric

1 yard (1m) of binding fabric

White cotton thread for piecing and quilting

Basic kit (see page 8)

Seam roller (optional)

Finished size

73 x 76in (185.5 x 193cm)

This quilt was made using fabrics from Libs Elliots's line from Andover Fabrics called "Wildside." The batting (wadding) used is Warm and Natural, supplied by The Warm Company. The threads used for piecing and quilting are from Aurifil.

Cutting

Press all fabrics for the quilt top before cutting for easier piecing. Use the cutting list below for the size and quantity of each piece. See page 10 for how to cut accurate squares. Copy the templates on page 123, following the instructions on page 15.

Pink: Cut ten 4-in (10-cm) squares and three 11-in (28-cm) squares

Yellow: Cut ten 4-in (10-cm) squares and three 11-in (28-cm) squares

Green: Cut ten 4-in (10-cm) squares and three 11-in (28-cm) squares

Blue: Cut ten 4-in (10-cm) squares and three 11-in (28-cm) squares

Light cream/white: Cut 160 triangles using Template A

Light cream/white: Cut 160 triangles using Template B and 160 with template B reversed

Dark gray/black: Cut 160 triangles using Template A

Dark gray/black: Cut 160 triangles using Template B and 160 with template B reversed

1 To create each of the eight triangle blocks for the 9-patch blocks you will need a Template A, a Template B, and a Template B reversed.

2 Place the right-hand B triangle RS together on the A triangle. Pin if needed and carefully sew with a ¼in (6mm) seam allowance. Press the seam. Repeat to add the other triangle B on the left side.

3 Repeat steps 1 and 2 to make another seven identical triangle blocks. Position the eight small triangle blocks and one color print square as shown. Begin your 9-patch by piecing each row together.

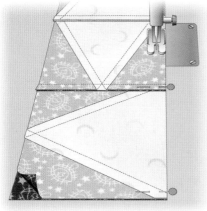

4 Then align the seams and points, pinning along the rows, and stitch the rows together.

5 Repeat steps 1 to 4 to make a total of 20 dark background 9-patch blocks and 20 light background 9-patch blocks. Arrange the blocks on your design wall (or floor) in rows on point, following the photograph on page 72 as a guide.

Backing, quilting, and binding

Make a quilt sandwich (see page 18) from your backing fabric (RS facing down), the batting (wadding), and the quilt top (RS facing up). Make sure all the layers are nice and smooth, with no wrinkles. Baste (tack) all three layers together, using safety pins or your preferred method.

Quilt as you prefer—I decided to quilt this project using my free-motion foot and free-motion quilting.

Prepare the binding and bind the edges of the quilt as described on pages 21–25.

6 Take the 11-in (28-cm) squares of print fabric and cut them once diagonally from point to point to make the triangle fillers for the ends of the rows. You will have one triangle in each color left over.

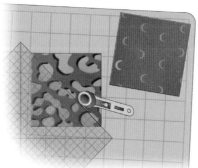

7 To complete the quilt top, simply join the blocks in each row together as you would normally. Note that the blocks in this quilt are set on point (see photograph above). Row 1 consists of the two large blue and green triangles in the top left corner; row 2 consists of one blue triangle, two 9-patch blocks, and one green triangle; and so on. Finish by joining the rows together.

Here Comes the Sun Mini Quilt

I have always had a fear of doing "Y" seams—I like to be exact and to the point about things, so not finishing the seam never sat right with me. Then I stumbled across this tile design and thought I could use this as the push to embrace my fear.

You will need

Fat quarter bundle

46½ x 49in (118 x 124cm) of batting (wadding)

2 yards (1.85m) of backing fabric

½ yard (0.45m) of binding fabric

White cotton thread for piecing and quilting

Basic kit (see page 8)

Seam roller (optional)

Finished size

44½ x 47in (113 x 119cm)

This quilt was made using fabrics from Annie Brady's line from Moda, called "Yucatan." The batting (wadding) used is Warm and Natural, supplied by The Warm Company. The threads used for piecing and quilting are from Aurifil.

Cutting

Press all fabrics from the bundle for easier cutting and piecing. Use the cutting list below for the size and quantity of each piece. Copy the templates on page 122, following the instructions on page 15. I used a belt hole maker to cut out the circles on Template A needed for the "Y" seaming. Don't forget this part!

Fat quarters: cut 40 using Template A and 40 using Template B

1 Using a sharp quilter's pencil or pen, mark a dot through the circles on Template A to establish the starting and stopping points on the reverse side of each piece of fabric.

TIP

When using templates I like to measure the height and cut my fabric into strips of that height to make cutting go a bit faster, so after squaring the fabrics, cut them into 5½-in (13.5-cm) wide strips.

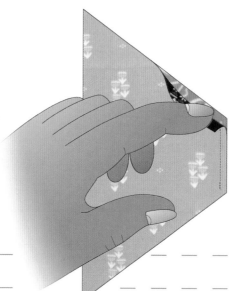

2 Place two Template A trapezoids RS up, with the short sides in the middle. Flip the right-hand one over onto the left-hand one, aligning the edges, and start the seam at the first dot, using a ¼-in (6-mm) seam allowance and backstitching to lock the threads. Sew to the second dot, backstitching again. Press the seam open.

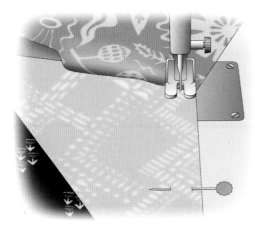

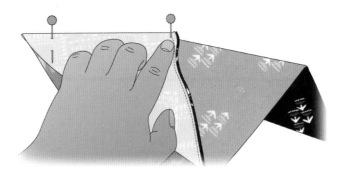

3 Position two Template B triangles in the openings of the joined trapezoids. Flip over the top triangle to align it with the right-hand side and pin the fabrics together along the seam. When you get to the middle seam you will need to fold back the other trapezoid so you have access to the starting dot. Transfer to the machine and, using the hand wheel, turn the needle to the down position right on the starting dot on the middle seam. Sew to the end of the seam.

4 Pivot the triangle to align along the second side and pin. Again starting at the middle seam, position the needle on the starting dot and sew to the end of the seam.

5 Repeat with the second triangle and then press your block. Repeat to make 20 finished blocks, following the photograph opposite for color position.

6 Position the blocks in five rows of four blocks, following the photograph opposite for layout. Piece the blocks together in rows as you would normally, with a ¼-in (6-mm) seam allowance.

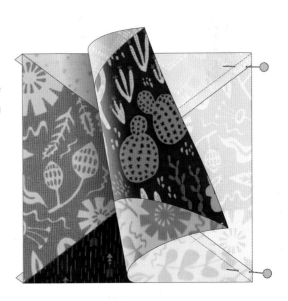

7 Press the odd-row seams to the left and the even-row seams to the right to help with nesting the seams (see page 17). Then sew the rows together and press these seams open.

Backing, quilting, and binding

Make a quilt sandwich (see page 18) from your backing fabric (RS facing down), the batting (wadding), and the quilt top (RS facing up). Make sure all the layers are nice and smooth, with no wrinkles. Baste (tack) all three layers together, using safety pins or your preferred method.

Quilt as you prefer—I decided to quilt this project with a small grid using gently curving lines.

Prepare the binding and bind the edges of the quilt as described on pages 21–25.

I once saw an old book jacket that was designed back in the fifties and it has intrigued me ever since. It was in French so I didn't understand it, but the cover was appealing. When I was working at Penguin I would periodically skim through the older book covers for inspiration and this one always found its way back into my mind.

Orbie Quilt

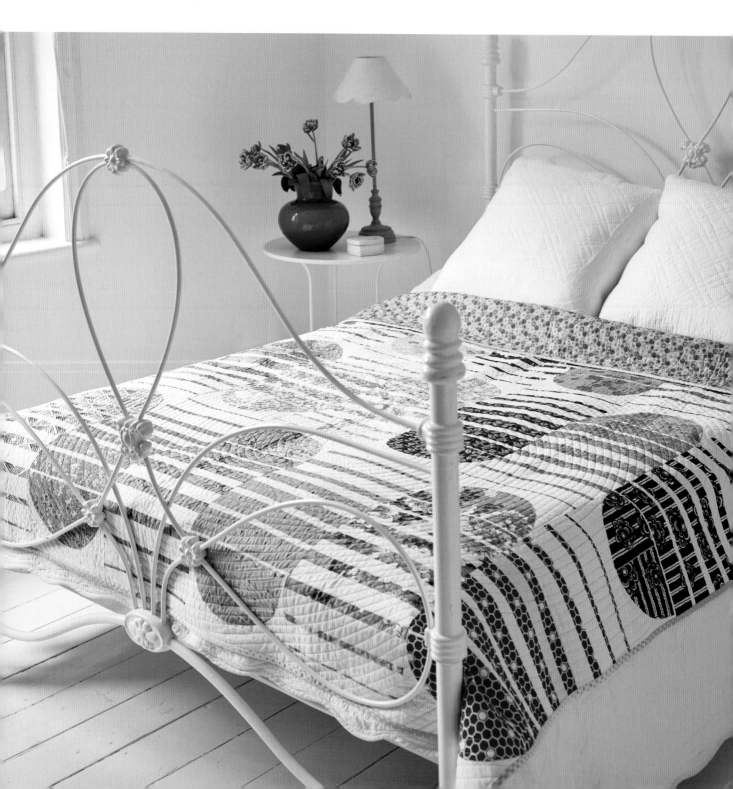

You will need

21 fat quarters

4 yards (3.65m) of various white tone-on-tone fabrics

74⅞ x 77¼in (190 x 196cm) of batting (wadding)

5 yards (4.8m) of backing fabric

½ yard (0.45m) of binding fabric

White cotton thread for piecing and quilting

Basic kit (see page 8)

Seam roller (optional)

Finished size

68⅞ x 71¼in (175 x 181cm)

This quilt was made using fabrics from my stash. The batting (wadding) used is Warm and Natural, supplied by The Warm Company. The threads used for piecing and quilting are from Aurifill.

Cutting

Press all fabrics for the quilt before cutting for easier piecing. Square up the outer edges of the fat quarter before trimming out your pieces. Use the cutting list below for the size and quantity of each piece. Copy the templates on page 124, following the instructions on page 15.

Each fat quarter: Cut a 2½ x 11-in (6.5 x 28-cm), a 2¼ x 11-in (5.75 x 28-cm), a 2 x 11-in (5 x 28-cm), a 1¾ x 11-in (4.5 x 28-cm), a 1½ x 11-in (4 x 28-cm), a 1¼ x 11-in (3.25 x 28-cm), a 1 x 11-in (2.5 x 28-cm) and a ¾ x 11-in (18mm x 28-cm) strip, then cut two quarter-circles using Template A

White fabric: Cut twenty-one each of 2½ x 11-in (6.5 x 28-cm), 2¼ x 11-in (5.75 x 28-cm), 2 x 11-in (5 x 28-cm), 1¾ x 11-in (4.5 x 28-cm), 1½ x 11-in (4 x 28-cm), 1¼ x 11-in (3.25 x 28-cm), 1 x 11-in (2.5 x 28-cm) and ¾ x 11-in (18mm x 28-cm) strips, 42 pieces using Template B, fourteen 1½ x10-in (4 x 26.5-cm) strips, and fourteen 2¼ x 10½-in (5.75 x 26.5-cm) strips

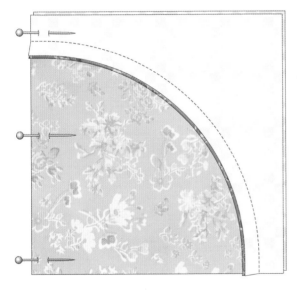

1 To create the curved section of the block, take the two quarter-circles in the same print and match them with the two outer white sections. Sew the curved seams. Press the seams and then join the two quarter-circle edges together with a ¼-in (6-mm) seam to make a half-circle in the print, press the seam open, and set aside.

2 Arrange a set of the same print and matching size white fabric strips. Start by placing the narrowest ¾in (18mm) print next to the widest 2½in (6.5cm) white fabric. As the width of the print strips increases, the white strips get narrower.

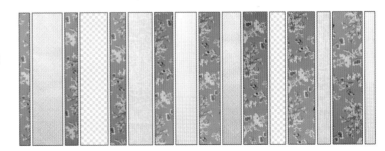

3 Align the long edge of the first pair of fabrics and sew, using a ¼-in (6-mm) seam allowance. Keep adding the remaining strips in the same way to complete the full striped section. Press the seams toward the colored prints so that they will not show through the white fabrics.

4 Once the fabric has all been pieced, it will need to be trimmed to the final dimension. The length can stay as it is, but the height will need to be trimmed to 10½in (26.5cm). To square up the edges on the half-circle place your quilter's ruler over the fabric, matching the quarter mark on the ruler along the bottom seam and the top center seam. Trim away the extra fabric and then rotate the fabric and ruler to trim the opposite sides. The final size should be 10½ x 5½in (26.5 x 14cm).

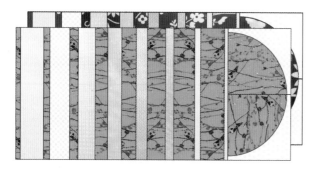

5 Place the squared-up half-circle unit next to the shortest white stripe, then flip over so they are RS together. Stitch together with a ¼-in (6-mm) seam allowance and press the seam toward the circle. Repeat all the steps to make up the other print and white units.

6 Arrange the completed units on your design wall with three units in each of the seven rows, following the photograph opposite. The units in the first row will all face the same way, then in the next row they'll face the other way and so on. Add a 1½ x 10½-in (4 x 26.5-cm) white strip between the first and second and the second and third blocks in each row. Then add a 2¼ x 10½-in (5.75 x 26.5-cm) white strip to the beginning and end of every row. Attach the rows together with pins, and then sew with a ¼-in (6-mm) seam allowance.

7 Sew all the rows together with a ¼-in (6-mm) seam allowance to make up the quilt top.

Backing, quilting, and binding

Make a quilt sandwich (see page 18) from your backing fabric (RS facing down), the batting (wadding), and the quilt top (RS facing up). Make sure all the layers are nice and smooth, with no wrinkles. Baste (tack) all three layers together, using safety pins or your preferred method.

Quilt as you prefer—I quilted it in concentric circles radiating out from the center.

Prepare the binding and bind the edges of the quilt as described on pages 21–25.

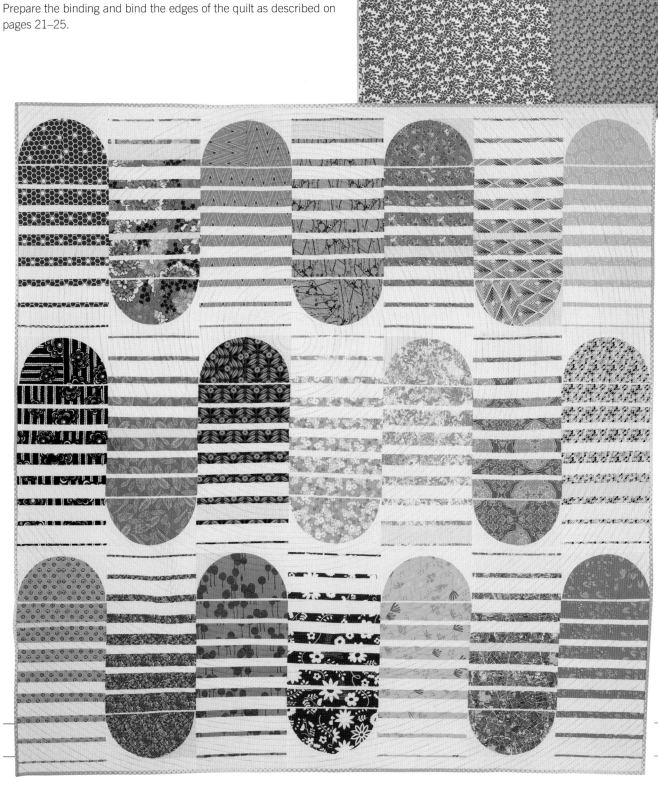

When I saw the brightly colored fabrics in this range, I immediately thought about kites in the sky. Then I remembered seeing an interesting wood floor when we were building our house. Who says you can't merge different things you see into one project!

Flying High Quilt

You will need

1 fat quarter bundle

50½ x 79in (128 x 203cm) of batting (wadding)

2 yards (1.85m) of backing fabric

½ yard (0.45m) of binding fabric

White cotton thread for piecing and quilting

Basic kit (see page 8)

Seam roller (optional)

Finished size

44½ x 74½in (113 x 189cm)

This quilt was made using fabrics from Sandy Gervais' range called "Well Said" from Moda Fabrics. The batting (wadding) used is Warm and Natural, supplied by The Warm Company. The threads used for piecing and quilting are from Aurifil.

Cutting

Press all fabrics for the quilt before cutting for easier piecing. Use the cutting list below for the size and quantity of each piece. Copy the templates on page 119, following the instructions on page 15.

Fat quarters: square up the long edge and cut a long 2½in (6.5cm) wide strip from each piece, then use Template A to cut 56 long triangles and Template B to cut 70 short triangles. Rotate your templates when marking, to minimize wasted fabric.

TIP

After squaring the fat quarters, I sometimes like to cut a 2-in (6.5-cm) wide strip to create a fun scrappy binding with the same fabrics I used on the quilt top.

1 Arrange the triangles on your design wall, using the photograph on page 82 as a guide. Make sure the colors match up so the sets of short and long triangles will form the kite shapes.

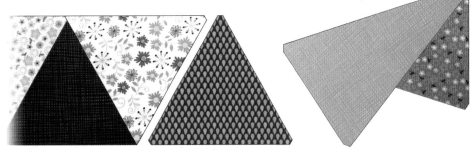

2 When you are ready to start attaching your rows, take the first three short triangles and place them in front of you. Take the middle triangle and place it RS together on the left triangle, aligning the right-hand edge. Pin and sew, using a ¼-in (6-mm) seam allowance.

3 Press the seam to the left and then attach the next triangle. Repeat until the first row is complete. Label as Row 1 and set aside.

4 To make the tall triangle rows, the process is the same. Place two triangles RS together, with the long edges aligned, and pin for sewing.

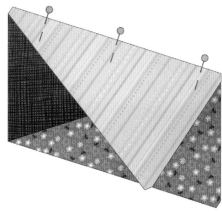

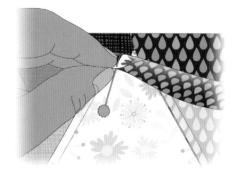

5 Sew using a ¼-in (6-mm) seam allowance. Press the seam to the left and then attach the next triangle. Work your way across the row, pressing the seam to the left each time.

6 When all of the rows have been completed, assemble them by inserting a pin through the point of a triangle and then match it with the matching point on the underside row. Pin at each seam point to ensure the corners line up.

7 Sew together using a ¼-in (6-mm) seam allowance and then press all the seams downward.

Backing, quilting, and binding

Make a quilt sandwich (see page 18) from your backing fabric (RS facing down), the batting (wadding), and the quilt top (RS facing up). Make sure all the layers are nice and smooth, with no wrinkles. Baste (tack) all three layers together, using safety pins or your preferred method.

Quilt as you prefer—I decided to quilt this project using my walking foot with a slightly longer stitch length of around 3.5mm, and to echo the shape of the kites. Once I had completed the long top-to-bottom quilted line I started again at the top, spacing the next stitched row by the width of the walking foot.

Prepare the binding and bind the edges of the quilt as described on pages 21–25.

For some reason I am really drawn to these geometric patterns. Being able to use simple piecing techniques to create the project allows me to have fun with the color and layouts. Clip the corners or "knot"—it's up to you!

Not a Celtic Knot Quilt

You will need

½ yard (0.45m) of light blue fabric

½ yard (0.45m) of dark blue fabric

⅔ yard (61cm) of orange fabric

¼ yard (25cm) of green fabric

¼ yard (25cm) brown fabric

2 yards (1.85m) of cream fabric

52 x 75¼in (132 x 191cm) of batting (wadding)

3 yards (2.75m) (horizontal) to 4 yards (3.65m) (vertical) of backing fabric (depending on direction of fabric pattern)

½ yard (0.45m) of binding fabric

Basic kit (see page 8)

Finished size

46 x 69¼in (117 x 176cm)

This quilt was made using fabrics from Jennifer Sampou's range called "Shimmer On" from Robert Kaufman Fabrics. The batting (wadding) used is Warm and Natural, supplied by The Warm Company. The threads used for piecing and quilting are from Aurifil.

Cutting

Press all fabrics for the quilt before cutting for easier piecing. Use the list chart below for the size and quantity of each piece.

Light blue fabric: cut seven 7½-in (19-cm) squares and nine 6½ x 4-in (16.5 x 10-cm) rectangles

Dark blue fabric: cut four 7½-in (19-cm) squares, seven 6½ x 4-in (16.5 x 10-cm) rectangles, and one 6½ x 24-in (16.5 x 61-cm) rectangle

Orange fabric: cut eight 7½-in (19-cm) squares, seven 6½ x 4-in (16.5 x 10-cm) rectangles, and one 6½ x 24-in (16.5 x 61-cm) rectangle

Green fabric: cut six 6½ x 4-in (16.5 x 10-cm) rectangles

Brown fabric: cut four 6½ x 4-in (16.5 x 10-cm) rectangles

Cream fabric: cut three 7½-in (19-cm) squares, twelve 4-in (10-cm) squares, six 4 x 18-in (10 x 46-cm) strips, four 4 x 24-in (10 x 61-cm) strips, two 4 x 32-in (10 x 81-cm) strips, four 6½ x 12-in (16.5 x 30.5-cm) strips, and six 6½ x 18-in (16.5 x 46-cm) strips

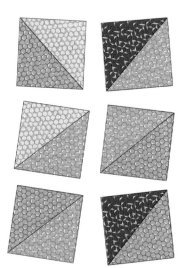

1 To create the HST blocks, you can use the double method (see page 12) for those with an even number of finished blocks. For those with an odd number of blocks, use the individual method (see page 11). You'll need four dark blue and light blue, seven brown and light blue, five brown and dark blue, three brown and cream and three cream and light blue.

2 Press the seams to the darker color before trimming to the final 6½-in (16.5-cm) square. Using the 45-degree marking on a large square ruler, align the seam along the mark and square up two sides, rotate 180 degrees, and trim to the final size.

3 You'll be piecing the rows on point. Arrange all the blocks on your design wall according to the photograph on page 84, adding 4-in (10-cm) cream squares between the rectangles. Begin sewing the blocks together in rows, using a ¼-in (6-mm) seam allowance.

4 Take the cream 4-in (10-cm) and 6½-in (16.5-cm) strips and add them to the beginning and end of each row. Row 1 is a single 4 x 32-in (10 x 81-cm) cream strip, row 2 has a 6½ x 12-in (16.5 x 30.5-cm) strip at the beginning and a 6½ x 18-in (16.5 x 46-cm) strip at the end, and row 3 has a 4 x 18-in (10 x 46-cm) strip at the beginning and a 4 x 24-in (10 x 61-cm) strip at the end.

5 Row 4 has the same cream strips as row 2, row 5 has the same as row 3, row 6 just has a 6½ x 12-in (16.5 x 30.5-cm) strip at the beginning, and row 7 has 4 x 18-in (10 x 46-cm) strip at each end. Row 8 has 6½ x 12-in (16.5 x 30.5-cm) strip at the end, row 9 has 4 x 24-in (10 x 61-cm) strip at the beginning and a 4 x 18-in (10 x 46-cm) strip at the end, row 10 has a 6½ x 18-in (16.5 x 46-cm) strip at the beginning and a 6½ x 12-in (16.5 x 30.5-cm) strip at the end, row 11 has the same as row 9, row 12 has the same as row 10, and row 13 is a single 4 x 32-in (10 x 81-cm) cream strip. Press the seams toward the darker fabric.

TIP

The fun part of this quilt was that it was created using the same pattern design from the "Shimmer On" range in six different colors.

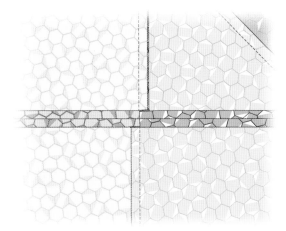

6 When all the rows are finished, match up the seams and pin to keep them in place before sewing the rows together with a ¼-in (6-mm) seam allowance, following the photograph as a guide. Press these seams open.

7 Once the quilt top is complete, take your 6½-in (16.5-cm) wide long quilter's ruler and, using the seams along the side, align and trim away the extra fabric strips. Repeat along the top and bottom, matching the edge of the ruler to the points.

Backing, quilting, and binding

Make a quilt sandwich (see page 18) from your backing fabric (RS facing down), the batting (wadding), and the quilt top (RS facing up). Make sure all the layers are nice and smooth, with no wrinkles. Baste (tack) all three layers together, using safety pins or your preferred method.

Quilt as you prefer—I decided to quilt this project using my walking foot and evenly spaced straight-line quilting.

Prepare the binding and bind the edges of the quilt as described on pages 21–25.

I wanted to see if I could take the standard Drunkards Path block and add my own spin to it by making it with double-sided curves. You can also create a pieced Orange Peel Quilt instead of appliqué. I used the templates designed by Jen Carlton Bailly in the 6½-in (16.5-cm) size for this quilt, but you can easily use any size to make it smaller.

Starlight Quilt

You will need

1½ yards (1.4m) of cream fabric

1½ yards (1.4m) of green fabric

1½ yards (1.4m) of blue fabric

1 yard (1m) of pink fabric

3¼ yards (3m) of backing fabric

56¼ x 56¼in (142.75 x 142.75cm) of batting (wadding)

½ yard (0.45m) of binding fabric

White thread for piecing and quilting

Basic kit (see page 8)

Glue stick (optional)

Seam roller (optional)

Finished size

51¼ x 51¼in (130 x 130cm)

This quilt was made using fabrics from Christa Watson's line from Benartrex Fabrics called "Modern Marks." The batting (wadding) used is Warm and Natural, supplied by The Warm Company. The threads used for piecing and quilting are from Aurifil.

Cutting

Press all fabrics for the quilt top before cutting for easier piecing. Use the cutting list below for the size and quantity of each piece. Copy the templates on page 124, following the instructions on page 15.

Cream: Cut 43 pieces using Template A, 8 pieces using Template B, and 2 pieces each 6½in (16.5cm) square

Green: Cut 4 pieces using Template A and 60 pieces using Template B

Blue: Cut 4 pieces using Template A and 60 pieces using Template B

Pink: Cut 28 pieces using Template A

1 I use a combination of pins and glue when making my curved blocks. Take a pink Template A piece and a green Template B and place them right sides up in front of you. Fold each piece in half to find the center of the curve. I prefer to fold one with RS together and the other with WS together so the center creases will nest together.

2 Flip the A unit onto the B unit and nest the creased fold. Align the edge and pin the two pieces together at the fold, taking up only a small bite of fabric. This will help allow the fabrics to twist and turn for proper seam alignment.

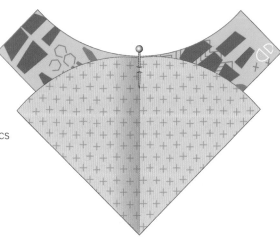

3 With a glue stick, put a few dabs of glue inside the ¼-in (6-mm) seam allowance along the curved edge of unit A, about ¼in (6mm) apart. The glue will act like pins and secure the fabrics for piecing. Take the matching outer squared corner on each unit and stick together, and then work your way down toward the center pin. Repeat with the other corner.

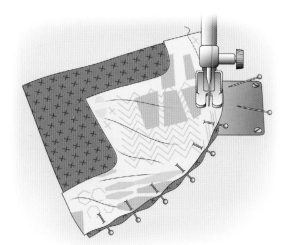

4 Carefully bring the glued pieces to your machine and sew with a ¼-in (6-mm) seam allowance along the curved edge. As you sew, smooth out any bubbles and puckers. When you get to the center pin, stop and remove it before finishing the curve.

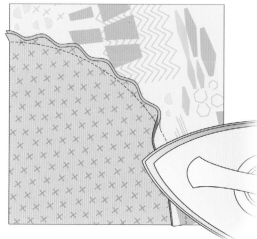

5 I prefer to press the seam to the inside so that, when I trim the blocks to the final size, the seam allowance is out of the way of future piecing.

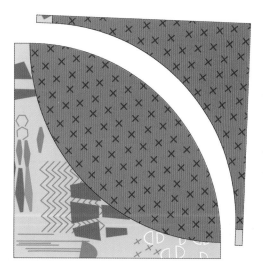

6 To create the second half of the block, position the larger curved side to the top and align Template A along the bottom left side. Trim away along the curve using a rotary cutter.

7 Take a blue B unit and fold it in half to find the center of the curve. Repeat steps 2 to 5 to attach the blue B unit to the new outer side of the block. Make another 27 blocks in the same colors, then make a further 21 blocks using a cream A piece with green and blue B pieces.

8 Repeat steps 1 to 5 to make 15 single curve blocks in cream and green and 15 in blue and cream, following the photograph on page 89 as a guide for color placement.

9 To square the double curve blocks to the final dimensions, place the corner of a large square quilter's ruler just to the outside of the intersection of the three fabrics. Move and adjust that position so the ¼-in (6-mm) mark on the ruler is directly above the intersection. Cut off the excess fabric so that, when you attach the blocks, the points will merge correctly.

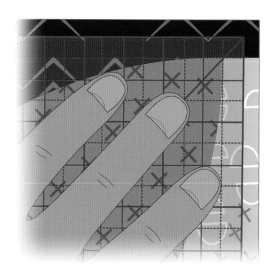

10 Square up the single curved block in the same way. Place your ruler so that both seams are positioned on the ¼-in (6-mm) marks on the ruler. Cut the 90-degree corner, then rotate the fabric and square the block to the final dimension using the two cut sides. All the blocks should be trimmed to 6½in (16.5cm) square.

11 Using the photograph below as a guide for the position of the blocks, take your first two and place them side by side. Flip over the right block so two blocks are RS together and pin along the edge. Sew with a ¼-in (6-mm) seam allowance.

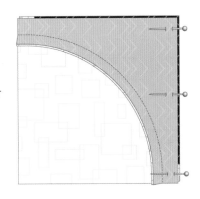

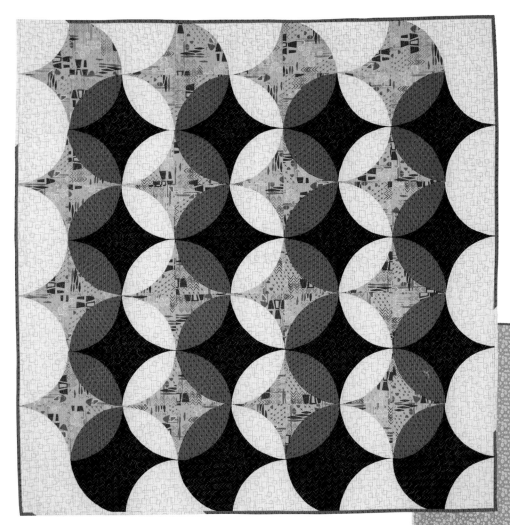

12 Repeat the assembly of the rows, pressing the seams on the odd rows to the left and those on the even rows to the right. Then join your rows together by pinning and sewing from the center of the row out to the sides.

Backing, quilting, and binding

Make a quilt sandwich (see page 18) from your backing fabric (RS facing down), the batting (wadding), and the quilt top (RS facing up). Make sure all the layers are nice and smooth, with no wrinkles. Baste (tack) all three layers together, using safety pins or your preferred method.

Quilt as you prefer— I decided to quilt this project using my walking foot and an echo-quilted diagonal grid of wavy lines (see page 20).

Prepare the binding and bind the edges of the quilt as described on pages 21–25.

Square Collision Quilt

Everyone knows the basic half-square triangle (HST) block, but you can take it up a notch by adding some more blocks and some sashing. HST quilts don't all have to look the same—you can use this versatile block in so many ways. Choose a bright charm pack and then a subtle, muted pack that work well together.

You will need

Two 5-in (12.5-cm) charm packs of contrasting prints

⅓ yard (30.5cm) fabric for sashing (if using)

35½ x 45in (90 x 114.25cm) of batting (wadding)

1¼ yards (1.15cm) of backing fabric

⅓ yard (30.5cm) of binding fabric

White cotton thread for piecing and binding

Basic kit (see page 8)

Seam roller (optional)

Finished size

29½ x 39in (75 x 99cm)

This quilt was made using fabrics from Zen Chic's range from Moda, called "Reel Time." The batting (wadding) used is Warm and Natural, supplied by The Warm Company. The threads used for piecing and quilting are from Aurifil.

Cutting

Press all fabrics for the quilt top before cutting for easier piecing. Use the cutting list below for the size and quantity of each piece.

Print fabrics: cut each into a 5-in (12.5-cm) square

Sashing: Cut 1½in (4cm) x WOF strips

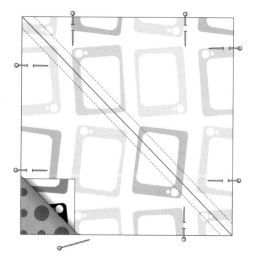

1 From your two packs of charm squares, pull out two contrasting prints and place them on your cutting mat RS up. On the lighter of the two fabrics, draw a diagonal line with a pen or pencil (it doesn't need to be a quilter's pencil) from one corner to the opposite corner.

2 Align the two fabrics with RS together. Using your machine with a ¼-in (6-mm) foot, sew down one side of the drawn line, placing the side of your foot along the line. Repeat on the second side.

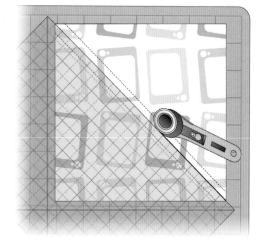

3 With your ruler and rotary cutter, cut along the drawn line to create two HST blocks. Open out the pieces and press your seams toward the darker fabric.

4 Place a second contrasting square from the pack RS down on one HST block and repeat the process of drawing a diagonal line on the new fabric, placing it perpendicular to the HST seam. Pin and sew as you did before.

5 Cut and press the new block. Repeat steps 1 to 5 until you have 68 blocks made up of a large triangle with two smaller triangles. Then repeat steps 1 to 3 to make 14 basic HST blocks—you'll only use 13 of these.

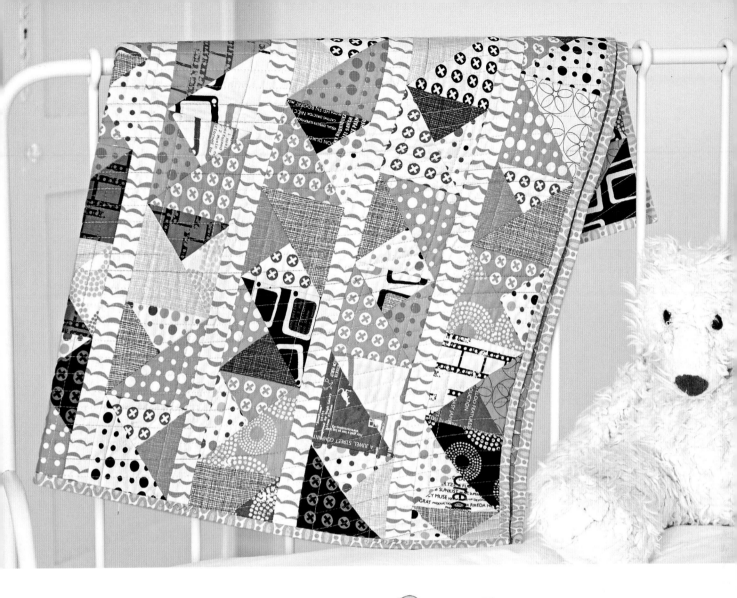

6 To square your basic HST block, use the diagonal 45-degree mark on the ruler and cut off the first corner, rotate, and repeat on the opposite side. To square up the other blocks, place your ruler on the block and align the 45-degree diagonal marking on the ruler with the long HST seam. Position the ruler so the 2-in (5-cm) mark is in the center, where the three fabrics meet. Cut the extra fabric away and then rotate the block 180 degrees to square the opposite side. Now line up your ruler with the 4-in (10-cm) marks and cut.

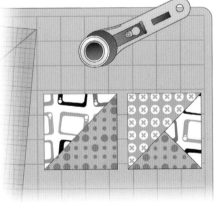

7 Lay out nine rows of nine blocks for a total of 81 blocks using, the photograph on page 92 as a guide. When you are satisfied with the arrangement, stack the blocks from row one by placing the left block over the right block and working your way from left to right.

8 Place the first two blocks side by side, flip one over so they are RS together, and then join using a ¼-in (6-mm) seam allowance. Keep adding a new block to the joined units until the row is complete.

TIP

To make a properly random quilt top, I prefer to place all of the blocks in a basket or bag and randomly pull to lay out the rows. You can always adjust the position of blocks if the colors are too similar in one section of the top.

9 When all of the rows are pieced and pressed, you can decide to join them as is or shift all the even rows to the left by half a block, as I have done (see above). You can then join as is with the stagger, or add horizontal sashing between the rows.

10 To add the sashing, sew a strip to the top of each row before sewing the rows together, using a ¼-in (6-mm) seam allowance each time. To attach the rows in the correct location for the staggered look, you will need to mark the halfway point of a HST block on an odd row at the opposite edge of attached sashing, so that you can line this mark up with the center seam between blocks on the next even row.

Backing, quilting, and binding

Make a quilt sandwich (see page 18) from your backing fabric (RS facing down), the batting (wadding), and the quilt top (RS facing up). Make sure all the layers are nice and smooth, with no wrinkles. Baste (tack) all three layers together, using safety pins or your preferred method.

Quilt as you prefer— I decided to quilt this project using my walking foot and horizontal parallel lines, and then added echo-quilted vertical lines (see page 20) that are slightly wavy.

Prepare the binding and bind the edges of the quilt as described on pages 21–25.

The New Divide Quilt

We all have a layer cake in our collection of fabric and we all have the same problem: what do I do with it? I get that question all the time! This is a simple pattern using every bit of a full layer cake.

You will need

10-in (25.5-cm) layer cake (42 pieces)

3½ yards (3.2m) of backing fabric

55 x 60in (140 x 152cm) of batting (wadding)

½ yard (0.45m) of binding fabric

Basic kit (see page 8)

Finished size

55¾ x 65in (141 x 164.5cm)

This quilt was made using one layer cake from the One Canoe Two line from Moda Fabrics called "Midnight Garden." The batting (wadding) used is Warm and Natural, supplied by The Warm Company. The threads used for piecing and quilting are from Aurifil.

Cutting

Press all fabrics for the quilt top before cutting for easier piecing. Each 10-in (25.5-cm) square will be cut in the same way—you can even stack them and cut multiples at the same time.

Cut each square into three identical pieces: a left triangle, a center 2-in (5-cm) wide strip, and a right triangle.

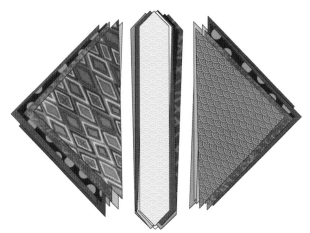

1 To make this a completely random quilt design, I placed each of the three sections in a separate bag and pulled one randomly from each to make up each square. Stack the pieces, ready to use.

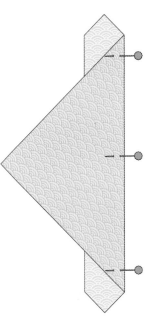

2 Start with your center strip RS up and place your right triangle RS down on top, centered and with the long edge aligned, and pin in place. Sew with a ¼-in (6-mm) seam allowance.

3 Add the left triangle in the same way. Press the seams toward the outer triangles. At this point, you can either square up the blocks and assemble them as is or move on to the next step.

4 Cut each square diagonally from point to point at right angles to the center stripe. Again using the random piecing method, grab two triangle halves and rejoin them into a square by pinning them from the center out to the corners and sewing with a ¼-in (6-mm) seam allowance. Trim each to the final size of 9½-in (24-cm) square.

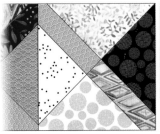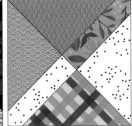

5 Lay out the 42 blocks in seven rows of six blocks, using the photograph opposite as a guide. Alternate the direction of the center strip so they can meet in the middle when the rows are joined.

6 Pin and sew the blocks together, using a ¼-in (6-mm) seam allowance. Then join your rows together by pinning and sewing from the center of the row out to the sides.

Backing, quilting, and binding

Make a quilt sandwich (see page 18) from your backing fabric (RS facing down), the batting (wadding), and the quilt top (RS facing up). Make sure all the layers are nice and smooth, with no wrinkles. Baste (tack) all three layers together, using safety pins or your preferred method.

Quilt as you prefer— I decided to quilt this project using my walking foot and an echo-quilted diagonal grid of wavy lines (see page 20).

Prepare the binding and bind the edges of the quilt as described on pages 21–25.

I don't know about you, but sometimes when it is stormy out I like to sit out on the porch and watch the rain come down. Seeing the movement and feeling the breeze. The Downpour Quilt is my representation of the rain falling with force.

Downpour Quilt

You will need

1 fat quarter bundle

45 x 70in (114.25 x 178cm) of batting (wadding)

2 yards (1.85m) of backing fabric

½ yard (0.45m) of binding fabric

Basic kit (see page 8)

Finished size

39 x 62in (99 x 157.5cm)

This quilt was made using fabrics from Betsy Siber's range called "Everglades" from Michael Miller Fabrics. The batting (wadding) used is Warm and Natural, supplied by The Warm Company. The threads used for piecing and quilting are from Aurifil.

Cutting

Press all fabrics for the quilt before cutting for easier piecing. Use the cutting list below for the size and quantity of each piece.

Fat quarter fabrics: cut into 2½ x 18in (6.5 x 46cm) strips.

Trim both ends of 59 strips with the angle leaning to the left and 53 with the angle on both ends leaning to the right.

> ### TIP
>
> Most fat quarters should be slightly larger than 18in (46cm) on the shorter side. Square up the edge and cut from that side. To speed up the cutting process, simply stack your fat quarters along the selvage edge and cut as a unit. I like to cut four fabrics at a time. Any more than that and the fabric has a tendency to shift.

1 To create the long rows, position two fabrics with the end cut going in the same direction.

2 Flip the right-hand strip over by 45 degrees and align both the corners and the diagonal seam edge. Pin in place and then sew, using a ¼-in (6-mm) seam allowance.

3 Open out and press the seam toward the darker fabric. Make up each row, using the photograph on page 98 as a guide, and then label the rows 1 through 37.

4 I find it easier to start with the longest rows, so start with rows 21 and 22. Position the two rows on your work surface and arrange them so that the short vertical seams of row 21 are centered on the long sections of row 22. You can find the center of the long seam by folding it in half and pressing the edge with your finger, leaving a small indication of where to match the seam. Pin along the row edge and sew using a ¼-in (6-mm) seam allowance.

5 To add row 23 to row 22, you will need to use your quilter's ruler and align the ruler's edge with the vertical seam from row 21. Every odd-numbered row must have the vertical seams aligned in this design.

6 To align the even rows, you will need to mark in the seam allowance on the edge of the previous odd-numbered row. Take your ruler and place the long edge across the points of the previous even-numbered rows. Take a pencil and put a mark in the seam allowance of the previous odd-numbered row. Align this mark with a diagonal seam or end on the next even-numbered row.

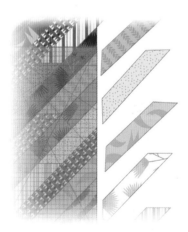

7 Continue joining rows in this way until you have made up the complete quilt top. Trim off the excess strips along each side and the bottom to straighten up the edges.

Backing, quilting, and binding

Make a quilt sandwich (see page 18) from your backing fabric (RS facing down), the batting (wadding), and the quilt top (RS facing up). Make sure all the layers are nice and smooth, with no wrinkles. Baste (tack) all three layers together, using safety pins or your preferred method.

Quilt as you prefer—I decided to quilt this project using my free-motion foot and free-motion quilting.

Prepare the binding and bind the edges of the quilt as described on pages 21–25.

Haydn's Quilt

Making a quilt doesn't always need to have 20 different prints to look cool. On a vacation to San Francisco many years ago, I remember seeing this pretty amazing installation using black and white tiles and three different shades of grout. The sharp contrast in the tiles looked completely different depending on which color grout was used. The same principle can be applied to quilting.

You will need

3 yards (2.75m) of solid dark blue fabric

3 yards (2.75m) of solid light blue fabric

1½ yards (1.4m) of solid orange fabric

72 x 90in (183 x 228.5cm) of batting (wadding)

4¾ yards (4.4m) of backing fabric

½ yard (0.45m) of binding fabric

White cotton thread for piecing and quilting

Basic kit (see page 8)

Seam roller (optional)

Finished size

62 x 82in (157.5 x 208cm)

This quilt was made using fabrics from Robert Kaufman's Kona Solid line and Michael Miller's "Herd" from their Trekking collection. The batting (wadding) used is Warm and Natural, supplied by The Warm Company. The threads used for piecing and quilting are from Aurifil.

Cutting

Press all fabrics for the quilt before cutting for easier piecing. Use the cutting list below for the size and quantity of each piece.

Dark blue fabric: cut seventeen 4½in (11.5cm) by WOF strips

Light blue fabric: cut eighteen 4½in (11.5cm) by WOF strips

Orange fabric: cut thirty-four 1½in (4cm) by WOF strips

1 To create the alternating dark/light groups, sew together a 4½-in (11.5-cm) dark and a 4½-in (11.5-cm) light strip along one long edge, using a ¼-in (6-mm) seam allowance. You will need to do this 17 times. Press the seam toward the darker fabric and set aside.

2 When all of the long rows have been sewn together, you can sub-cut them into 4½ x 8½-in (11.5 x 21.5-cm) rectangles. Press the seams toward the darker fabric. Each row will require eight sets of rectangles, which will be sewn together to make a row.

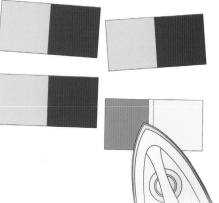

3 On rows 2, 3, 4, 6, 7, 8, 10, 11, 12, 14, 15, and 16, you will need to add an additional light 4½-in (11.5-cm) square to the beginning of each row to allow for the offset spacing.

4 Join together the short sides of two sashing pieces so the strip will be long enough to attach to the rows. Add the sashing to the bottom of each of the 17 rows, then cut off the excess fabric from the sashing.

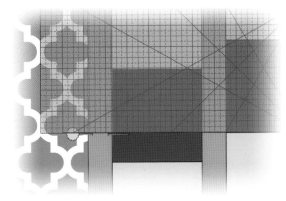

5 To get the offset effect, on the first light square of the first row use your quilter's ruler to measure 1⅜in (3.5cm) from the seam. Place a pin in the sashing. Position the seam between the first dark and second light square on the second row over the pin. Then sew the rows together using a ¼-in (6-mm) seam allowance.

6 Repeat the same measuring and pinning for the third row, this time measuring on the first dark square of the second row and aligning the seam between the first light and dark squares on the third row on the pin. Sew the row together. On the fourth row you will need to match the seams with the second row positioning. Row 5 will match row 1 and so on—follow the photograph on page 100 for the alignment of each row.

Backing, quilting, and binding

Make a quilt sandwich (see page 18) from your backing fabric (RS facing down), the batting (wadding), and the quilt top (RS facing up). Make sure all the layers are nice and smooth, with no wrinkles. Baste (tack) all three layers together, using safety pins or your preferred method.

Use your walking foot to sew through the layers, making a smooth gentle curve from top to bottom. I used a dark blue thread for the darker blocks and a lighter blue for the others.

Prepare the binding and bind the edges of the quilt as described on pages 21–25.

chapter 3

home DECOR

Making a placemat set as a gift for someone is a fun way to use up some of your stash fabric. Even something that just catches the crumbs from your meal can have a bit of style. "Y" seams (or point-to-point sewing) isn't hard to do—it just takes a bit of planning and some stitching.

"Y" Me Placemat and Coaster

You will need for each placemat and matching coaster

Fat quarter of cream fabric

Fat eighth each of 2 different light color blue/yellow/red fabrics

Fat eighth each of 2 different medium color blue/yellow/red fabrics

18 x 21in (46 x 53.25cm) of batting (wadding)

Fat quarter of backing fabric

White cotton thread for piecing and quilting

Basic kit (see page 8)

Seam roller (optional)

Finished size

Placemat 14¼ x 19¼in (36 x 49cm)

Coaster 4⅞in (12.25cm) square

These placemats and coasters were made using fabrics from Sharon Holland's line from Art Gallery Fabrics called "Bountiful." The batting (wadding) used is Warm and Natural, supplied by The Warm Company. The threads used for piecing and quilting are from Aurifil.

Cutting

Press all fabric for the mats before cutting for easier piecing. Use the cutting list on the right for size and quantity of each piece. See page 10 for how to cut accurate squares. Copy the templates on page 125, following the instructions on page 15. I used a belt hole maker to cut out the corner circles needed for the "Y" seaming. Don't forget this part!

For each placemat and coaster

Cream fabric: Cut thirteen 2½-in (6.5-cm) squares

Light color fabric 1: Cut seven using template A with the RS up

Light color fabric 2: Cut seven using template A with the RS up

Medium color fabric 1: Cut seven using template A with the WS up

Medium color fabric 2: Cut seven using template A with the WS up

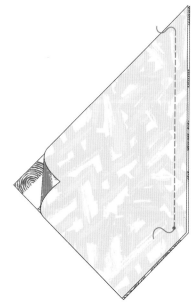

1 Using the templates, mark a dot through the corner circle on the WS of each fabric shape to indicate where you will be starting or stopping your stitching. A pencil with a sharp point is a good option here. Position the fabrics needed to complete one block RS up in front of you.

2 Place the two patterned fabric shapes RS together, with the long seam edge aligned. Carefully bring the fabric to your machine and, starting at the point, sew a scant ¼-in (5-mm) seam allowance—making sure to stop stitching when you reach the dot marked on the wrong side of the fabric.

3 Remove the fabric from the machine and fold the top fabric over. Because you stopped shy of the end of the seam, you will be able to fold the top layer over with the edge parallel to the bottom layer.

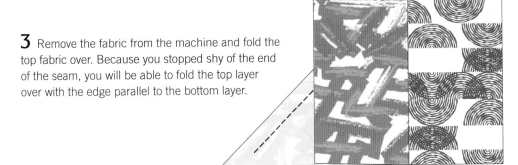

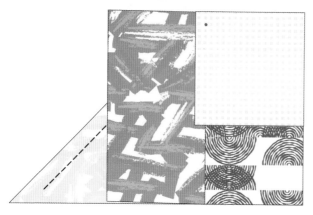

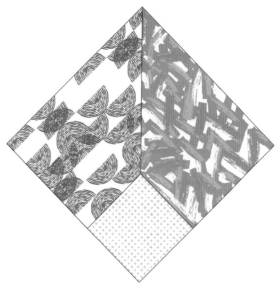

4 Place the small square cream fabric RS down on top, with the marked dot over the seam of the fabrics below. That dot will be your starting point to stitch.

5 Make sure to drop the needle as close to the dot as possible; doing so will help to eliminate any gap when the pieces are folded open and pressed. Stitch from the dot and off the end of the square to join the square to the blue fabric.

6 Refold the piece and swivel the square around to align the unstitched side with the edge of the other fabric shape. Be sure to move the folded section away from the stitching line. Stitch the seam from the dot again. Press the fabrics flat with a hot iron. Make 11 more blocks the same for the placemat, and one for the coaster.

Layout diagrams

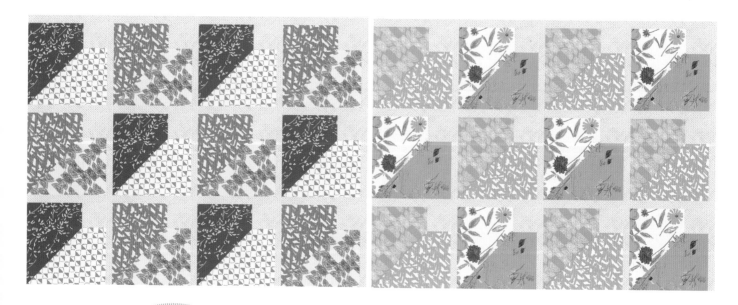

TIP

Use a seam roller to quickly press your fabric without having to get up and iron.

7 From the cream fabric, cut strips 1½in (4cm) x WOF for the two side sashes. I chain-pieced the blocks onto the sashing on the same side for all 13 blocks (see page xxx). I then cut them apart and chain-pieced the second side.

8 Press the sashing flat. Position and piece your placemat in three rows of four blocks, following the diagram above as a guide.

Backing and quilting

1 Measure the pressed placemat and coaster and cut a batting (wadding) layer and a backing layer to the same size for each. Make a sandwich (see page 18) from your backing fabric (RS facing down), the batting (wadding), and the placemat or coaster (RS facing up). Make sure all the layers are nice and smooth, with no wrinkles.

2 Along one of the short sides, place your hand close to the edge and place marker pins on either side of your hand. You will not be stitching between the marker pins as you will need a space to turn the placemats to the right side. Pin around the rest of the edge, securing the layers.

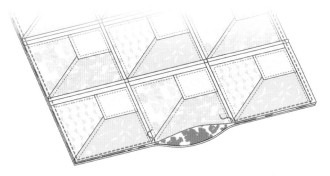

3 Carefully bring your pinned layers to your machine. After adjusting your seam allowance to approximately ½in (12mm), begin stitching on the outside of the marker pins, backstitching at the beginning. Work your way around the entire placemat and backstitch at the last marker pin, taking care to leave the opening for your hand.

4 Clip the corners of the placemat before turning it RS out. Clipping will help reduce the bulk in the corners and eliminate the rounded points.

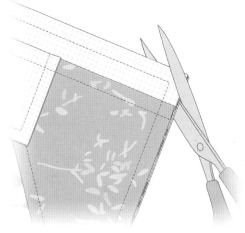

5 Reach inside the layers, between the top and the backing, and turn RS out through the hole left in the outside edge. At the opening, turn in the edges and fingerpress a ½-in (12-mm) seam allowance, then adjust your needle position and topstitch around the entire edge.

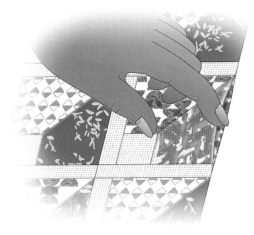

6 I adjusted my needle position and stitch length before starting my echo square spiral. Starting at one corner I stitched down the outside edge, stopping before I reached the next edge. With the needle down, I turned the placemat to align the next edge and then repeated the process until I made it to the center. Back and quilt the coaster in the same way.

Rubik's Cube Door Stop

When spring rolls around we like to leave the door to the screen porch open, but on breezy days we need something to keep it open. Nobody said a door stopper needed to be boring! We all have stash fabric in our collection that we just don't know what to do with, so take a few small bits from each piece and incorporate it into this fun door stopper.

You will need

3-in (7.5-cm) square of each of 9 red fabrics

3-in (7.5-cm) square of each of 9 white fabrics

3-in (7.5-cm) square of each of 9 green fabrics

3-in (7.5-cm) square of each of 9 orange fabrics

3-in (7.5-cm) square of each of 9 blue fabrics

3-in (7.5-cm) square of each of 9 yellow fabrics

2in (5cm) x WOF of black fabric

1in (2.5cm) x WOF of gray fabric

25 x 45in (64 x 114.25cm) of batting (wadding)

White cotton thread for piecing and quilting

Basic kit (see page 8)

10–12oz (300–350g) bag of polyester fiber fill

2 plastic bags

Small funnel

4lb (2 kg) of rice

Finished size

14in (35.5cm) cube

The batting (wadding) used is Warm and Natural, supplied by The Warm Company. The threads used for piecing and quilting are from Aurifil.

Cutting

Press all fabric for the cube before cutting for easier piecing. Use the cutting list below for the size and quantity of each piece.

Cut one 3-in (7.5-cm) square from each of the 54 colored fabrics

Cut the black fabric into two 1-in (2.5-cm) wide strips

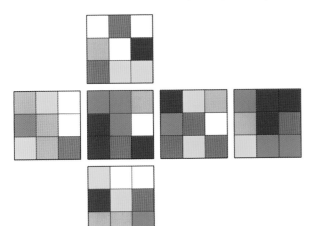

1 I wanted my Rubix Cube to look like it came out of a box all mixed up. I found a deconstructed image of a cube with all the random colors on the six sides. You can also make it with each side the same, or so it looks finished with matching colors.

2 Each side of the cube is a basic 9-patch unit. I added some sashing to it so it looked like frames around each spinning block. Place nine squares in front of you, right side up, using the color layout on one of the sides from the illustration above or an alternate configuration.

3 Take the squares from the left and center rows and chain piece (see page 17) them along their right-hand edge to the black sashing, using a ¼-in (6-mm) seam allowance. I like to position the squares as close as possible to the previous square when attaching them to eliminate extra trimming.

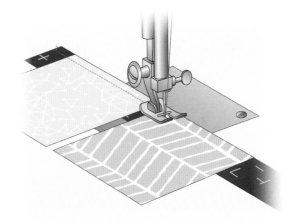

4 Once the six units have been separated and trimmed up if needed, position them back in the starting order.

5 Stitch the three units in each of the three rows together with a ¼-in (6-mm) seam allowance and then add the gray horizontal sashing between the first two rows.

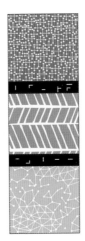
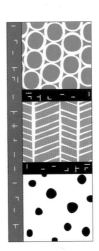
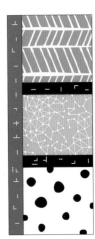

6 Add a black border around the four sides of the finished block.

7 Repeat steps 2 to 6 to make the remaining five sides of your Rubix Cube, following the diagram in step 1.

8 To add a bit of rigidity I pieced the four side blocks together into one long strip using a ½-in (12-mm) seam allowance, and then added a layer of batting (wadding) on the back. I then quilted some wavy lines along the sashing.

9 Place the cube top and bottom blocks on separate pieces of batting and repeat the same stitching. Square up all sides of the quilted sections.

11 Fold the cube up and align the remaining sides to the top, pinning as you adjust. Sew with the same ½-in (12-mm) seam allowance until the top is completely sewn to the sides.

10 Referring to the diagram on page 109, position the top of the cube RS together over the second side and pin in place. Stitch together using a ½-in (12-mm) seam allowance. I started and stopped stitching at the seam on the sides. Backstitch at both ends.

12 Add the bottom of the cube in the same way, but on the last open seam leave a 3–4in (7.5–10cm) opening to turn the cube right side out. Backstitch at both sides, as there will be a bit of tugging to turn out.

13 With the Rubix Cube RS facing out, push the polyester fiber fill firmly into the corners of the cube. Use about half of the fill.

14 To add a bit of weight to the door stop I inserted two plastic bags, one inside the other, into the middle of the cube and formed a void in the fiber fill for the rice. Using a small funnel, pour two 2-lb (1-kg) bags of rice into the plastic bag. Tie off the bags and push the knot back into the middle of the cube.

15 Stuff the remaining half bag of fiber fill around the rice, taking care to push out the corners of the cube. Stitch the opening firmly closed using a thick cotton thread.

I know I hate reaching for a pair of oven mitts to grab a hot tray out of the oven only to find just one! Using a quilt-as-you-go piecing method, you can knock out this double oven mitt just in time for dinner and never be single-handed in the kitchen again.

"Hot 2 Trot" Double Oven Mitt

You will need

Fat quarter of backing fabric

1½ yards (1.4m) of Insul-Bright heat-resistant batting (wadding)

⅓ yard (30.5cm) of various scrap fabrics for creating the top

Fat quarter of binding fabric

White cotton thread for piecing and quilting

Basic kit (see page xxx)

Finished size

8¼ x 36in (21 x 91.5cm)

This quilted oven mitt was made using fabrics from Maureen Cracknell's "Soulful" range from Art Gallery Fabrics. Insul-Bright thermal batting (wadding) is from the Warm Company. The threads used for piecing and quilting are from Aurifil.

Cutting

Press all fabric for the oven mitts before cutting for easier piecing. Use the cutting list below for the size and quantity of each piece.

Backing fabric: cut two 10-in (25.5-cm) squares

Scrap print fabrics: cut two 10-in (25.5-cm) squares, one 10 x 36-in (25.5 x 91.5-cm) rectangle and random strips 10in (25.5cm) long and ranging from 1in (2.5cm) to 3in (7.5cm) wide

Insul-Bright batting: cut two 10-in (25.5-cm) squares and one 10 x 36-in (25.5 x 91.5-cm) rectangle

Binding fabric: cut into 2½-in (6.5-cm) wide bias binding strips

1 Make a quilt sandwich (see page 18) with 10in (25.5cm) squares of print and backing fabric and the Insul-Bright batting, and quilt to secure the layers together. I used a gentle sweeping echo curve on both pieces. Repeat to make a second piece.

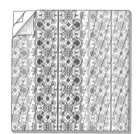

2 Bind one edge of each piece as described on pages 21–25. Use a plate measuring 8¼in (21cm) in diameter at the widest part to mark a curve in the center of the opposite end to the binding. With a sharp rotary cutter, trim the excess away from the curve and then continue down to trim the width of the whole piece to the diameter of the curve. Repeat on the second quilted piece. Set aside.

3 To keep the layers secure while you quilt-as-you-go, spray baste the 10 x 36-in (25.5 x 91.5-cm) rectangle of Insul-Bright to the WS of the same size piece of print fabric. Fold the basted layers in half to find the middle of the long sides.

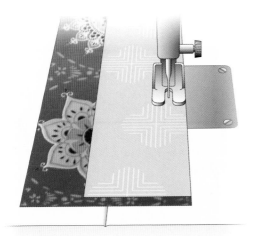

4 Take a 10in (25.5cm) strip and place it over the center fold line RS up, and then place a second fabric strip along the right-hand edge with RS facing down. Pin if you wish, and then sew through all the layers using a ¼in (6mm) seam allowance.

TIP

You can make the quilted side symmetrical as I have done, or use random colors and widths to personalize your project for yourself—or even for a friend.

5 Fold open the fabrics and press them flat. Continue adding strips on each side in this way until you have reached the ends.

6 When the quilt-as-you-go top is complete, measure and square it up to 8¼ x 36in (21 x 91.5cm). Use your circle template or plate to round off each end.

7 To make the hanging loop take a 2½ x 6-in (6.5 x 15-cm) strip of binding fabric and press it in half with WS together to create a center crease. Open flat, and then fold each long edge to the center crease and press. Refold along the center crease and press flat so that the raw edges are now hidden inside. Topstitch along the open side to secure it closed.

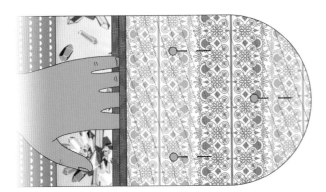

8 Take your hand sections made in step 2 and place them backing side down on the pieced side of the quilt-as-you-go top, matching up the curves at each end. Pin in place in several spots to help secure the two sections.

9 Place your hanging loop in the center of one of the long sides, aligning the raw ends to the outside edge. Pin as needed. Bind all round the edge as described on pages 21–25.

Love Hex Quilt

Every now and then I like to really challenge myself when designing a new quilt. I like to think I am more than capable of figuring easy ways to create difficult-looking designs and this was a pure test of my abilities. Getting all of the angles and sizes to match was a challenge, so it was drawn and redrawn several times. It is one of my favorites!

You will need

1½ yards (1.4m) of white background fabric

1 yard (1m) of pink fabric

1 yard (1m) of teal fabric

¾ yard (0.70m) of multi-colored fabric

46½ x 52 3/8in (118 x 133cm) of batting (wadding)

2½ yards (1.85m) of backing fabric

½ yard (0.45m) of binding fabric

White cotton thread for piecing and quilting

Basic kit (see page 8)

Finished size

40½ x 46½in (103 x 118cm)

This quilt was made using fabrics from Art Gallery Fabrics Capsules range called "Letter." The batting (wadding) used is Warm and Natural, supplied by The Warm Company. The threads used for piecing and quilting are from Aurifil.

Cutting

Press all fabrics for the quilt before cutting for easier piecing. Use the cutting list below for size and quantity of each piece. Copy the templates on pages 120–121, following the instructions on page 15. Take note to flip the templates as needed to obtain the correct orientation.

White fabric: Cut 20 pieces using Template B, 4 triangles using Template F, eight 4 x 13-in (10 x 33-cm) rectangles, and four 4in (10cm) x WOF strips

Pink fabric: cut 10 pieces using Template A with the RS up and 10 with the WS up, cut 8 pieces using Template C with the RS up and 8 with the WS up.

Teal fabric: cut 10 pieces using Template A with the RS up and 10 with the WS up, cut 8 using Template C with the RS up and 8 with the WS up.

Multi-colored fabric: cut 7 rectangles using Template E, 12 pieces using Template D, and 14 pieces using Template C

1 When all of your pieces are cut, you can arrange them on your worktable for assembly. To create the large diamond blocks, you will need to take a pair of Template A fabrics in each of pink and teal and a pair of white Template B fabrics. The diamond will need six pieces in total: two of the white Template B pieces, two pink Template C triangles (one facing each direction), and two of the teal Template A triangles (one facing each direction). To make the first half, flip the teal fabric RS together onto the white and join with a ¼-in (6-mm) seam allowance.

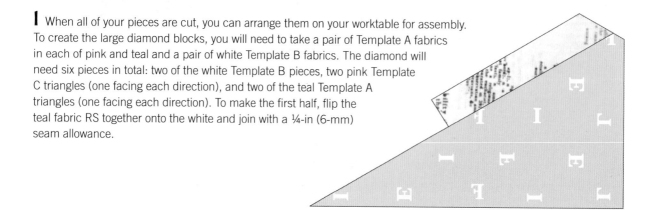

2 Then flip the pink fabric RS together onto the white and join with a ¼-in (6-mm) seam allowance. That is one half of the diamond.

3 Repeat the steps to make the second half of the block, and then join the two halves together with a ¼-in (6-mm) seam allowance. You'll need ten of these blocks in total.

Layout diagram

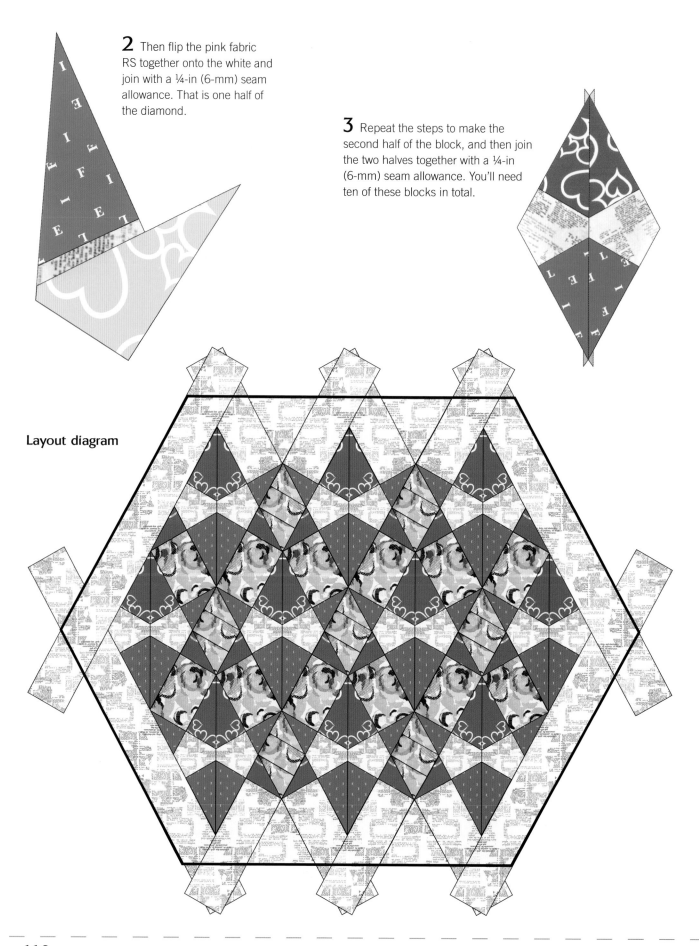

4 Use one multi-colored Template D fabric and a pink and a teal Template C triangle join to create the rhomboid block. You will need six of these in total.

5 Make seven Half Rectangles using the multi-colored fabric and teal Template C triangles, and seven using the multi-colored fabric and pink. Add a teal Template C triangle to one short edge of two of the 4in x 13-in (10 x 33-cm) rectangles, and a pink Template C triangle to one short edge of two more.

6 Once you have created all of the smaller pieces you can arrange them on your design wall (or floor) and fill in the missing sections with the remaining pieces, using the photograph on page 115 or the layout diagram on page 116 as a guide for positioning.

7 You'll be piecing the rows on point, again following the photograph or diagram. For the first diagonal row at top left, start by attaching a rhomboid to the top right edge of a diamond by aligning the matching seams and pin. Sew using a ¼-in (6-mm) seam allowance. Press and then add the bottom left edge of the second diamond to the other side of the rhomboid. At top right of the second diamond add a 4 x 13-in (10 x 33-cm) white rectangle with a teal end, then trim the excess from the plain end using the edge of the previous pieces as a guide. Finally add a Template F triangle.

8 For the next row, begin with a teal Template C triangle. Add a multi-color Template D, a pink and multi Half Rectangle, a Template E multi, and a teal and multi Half Rectangle. Repeat this sequence again, and then add a 4in x 13-in (10 x 33-cm) white rectangle at the top end.

9 Carry on in this way, following the diagram, until you have made all the diagonal rows. To join the diagonal rows you will need to match all the seams and pin along the sewn edge. First pin all the teal and pink seams, and then ease the middle fabric before pinning.

10 Add your final background frame of four 4-in (10-cm) WOF strips along the sides. Attach the first piece, then before sewing on the next piece use a ruler and rotary cutter to trim the end on the diagonal, using the edge of the quilt top as a guide.

Backing, quilting, and binding

Make a quilt sandwich (see page 18) from your backing fabric (RS facing down), the batting (wadding), and the quilt top (RS facing up). Make sure all the layers are nice and smooth, with no wrinkles. Baste (tack) all three layers together, using safety pins or your preferred method.

Quilt as you prefer—I decided to quilt this project using my walking foot and quilt gentle sweeping curves across the entire quilt. To do this I position my needle as far right as possible and use the left side of the walking foot along the previously stitched line.

Prepare the binding and bind the edges of the quilt as described on pages 21–25.

Templates

The templates in this section are printed at either 100% of their actual size or at 50% of their actual size. Those that are at 50% are clearly labeled and need to be enlarged by 200% using a photocopier or a scanner. See page 15 for more instructions on using templates.

Simple Fabric Boxes, page 28

For the small box: enlarge by 150%
For the medium box: enlarge by 200%
For the large box: enlarge by 250%

Cut two and join along the center for the full template

Flying High Quilt,
page 80—50% of actual size

A

B

Love Hex Quilt, page 114—
actual size

B

F

C

A

D

E

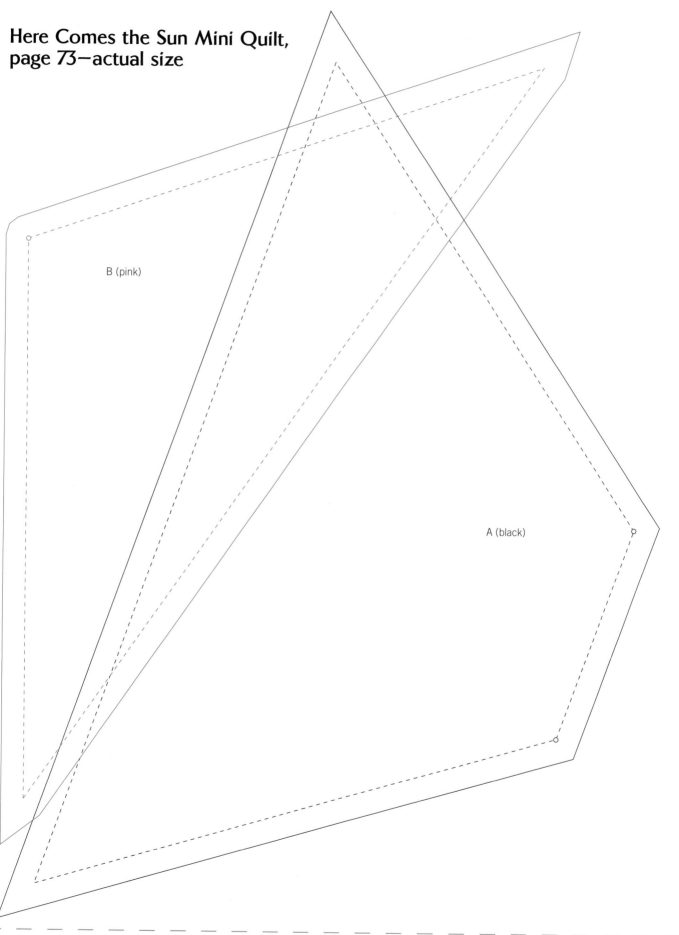

**Here Comes the Sun Mini Quilt,
page 73—actual size**

B (pink)

A (black)

Hyde Park Pouch, page 34—
50% of actual size

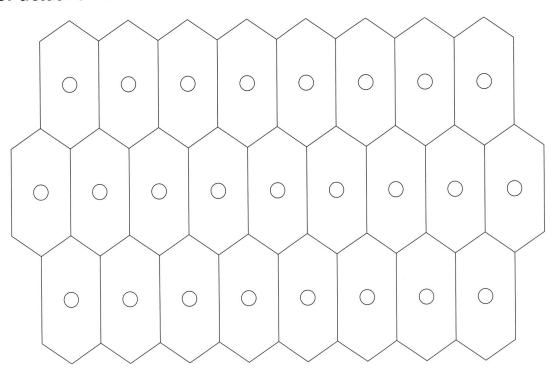

Hypno Quilt, page 70—
actual size

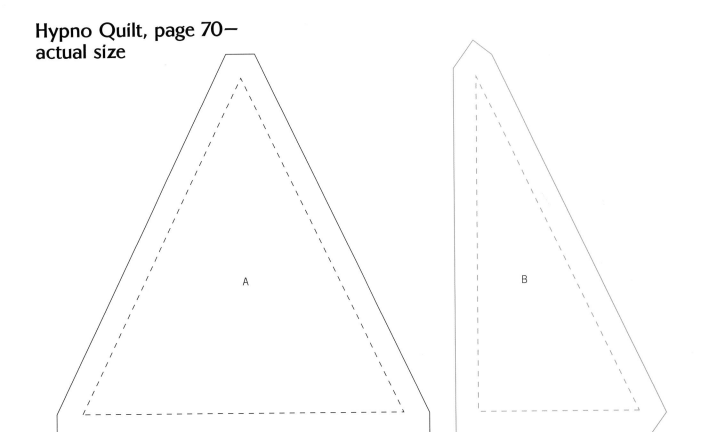

A

B

Orbie Quilt, page 76 and Starlight Quilt, page 86— actual size

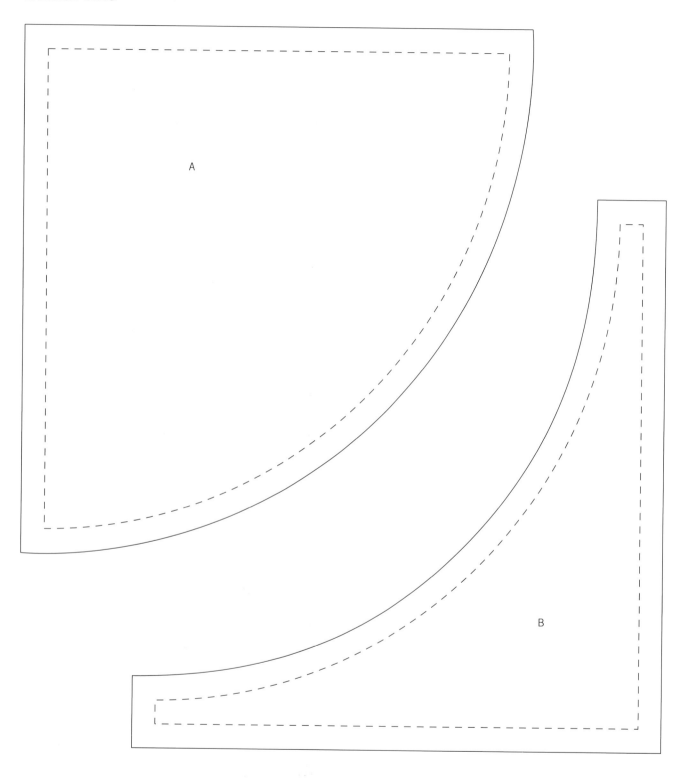

A

B

Color Wheel Mini Quilt, page 58—50% of actual size

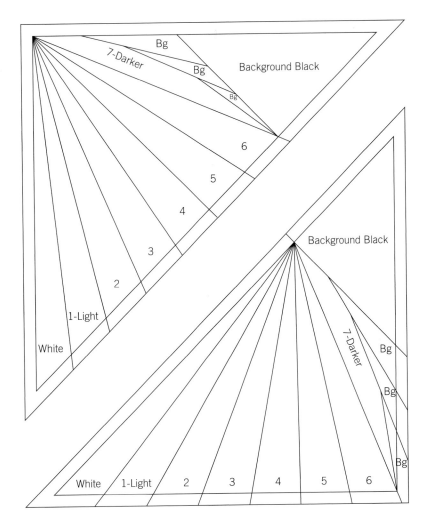

Bg
7-Darker
Bg
Bg
Background Black
6
5
4
3
2
1-Light
White

Background Black
7-Darker
Bg
Bg
Bg
White   1-Light   2   3   4   5   6

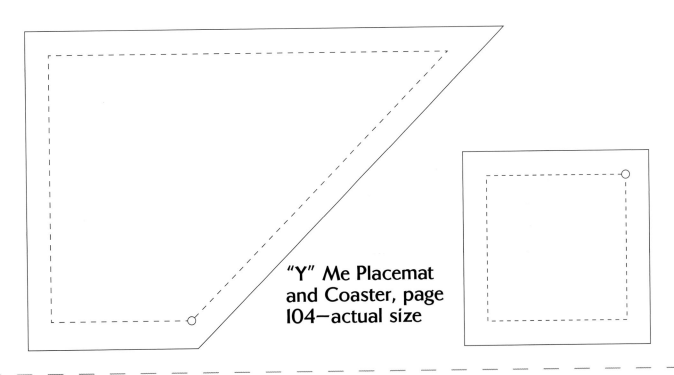

"Y" Me Placemat and Coaster, page 104—actual size

Suppliers

UK

The Village Haberdashery
Unit 6, Hardy Building
Heritage Lane
London NW6 2BR
Tel: 020 7624 5494
www.thevillagehaberdashery.
co.uk

Hobbycraft
www.hobbycraft.co.uk
(Stores nationwide)

The Cotton Patch
1283–1285 Stratford Road
Hall Green
Birmingham B28 9AJ
Tel: 0121 702 2840
www.cottonpatch.co.uk

Janome Sewing Machines
www.janome.com

John Lewis
www.johnlewis.com
(Stores nationwide)

Lady Sew and Sew
Moy House
Institute Road, Marlow
Bucks SL7 1BN
Tel: 01628 890 532
www.ladysewandsew.co.uk

Liberty of London
Regent Street
London W1B 5AH
Tel: 020 7734 1234
www.libertylondon.com

The Peacock and the Tortoise
29 George Street
Perth PH1 5LA
Tel: 01738 717009
www.thepeacockandthetortoise.
co.uk

RayStitch
66 Essex Road
London N1 8LR
Tel: 020 7704 1060
www.raystitch.co.uk

The Bramble Patch
West Street
Weedon
Northamptonshire NN7 4QU
Tel: 01327 342212
www.bramblepatchonline.com

The Quilt Room
36–39 High Street
Dorking
Surrey RH4 1AR
Tel: 01306 877307
www.quiltroom.co.uk

USA and Canada

Andover Fabrics
www.andoverfabrics.com

Art Gallery Fabrics
www.artgalleryfabrics.com

Aurifil Threads
www.aurifil.com

Benartex Fabrics
www.benartex.com

Cary Quilting Company
935 N Harrison Ave
Cary, NC 27513
Tel: 919 238 9739
www.caryquilting.com

The City Quilter
www.cityquilter.com
(Online store)

Fabric Depot
www.fabricdepot.com
(Online store)

The Fabric Worm
www.fabricworm.com
(Online store)

The Fat Quarter Shop
www.fatquartershop.com
(Online store)

Janome Sewing Machines
www.janome.com

Michael Miller Fabrics
www.michaelmillerfabrics.com

Michaels
www.michaels.com
(Stores nationwide)

Missouri Star Quilt Company
114 N Davis Street
Hamilton, MO 64644
Tel: 888 571 1122
www.missouriquiltco.com

Olfa
Rotary cutters and rulers
www.olfa.com

Robert Kaufman Fabrics
www.robertkaufman.com

The Warm Wadding Company
www.warmcompany.com

Index

Acknowledgments

Without question, I would like to thank my amazing wife Victoria for all the love and support she gives me when I am in work mode. I am sure it can be hard dealing with me when I am listening to my loud music and cutting up pretty fabrics! Thanks to our son Haydn for keeping me company on some of the days when he is not in pre-school and to my Mom and Dad for taking Haydn on the other days so I can work.

I would like to thank the team at Janome, both here in the US and also in the UK. Without your wonderful sewing machines I would be making everything by hand—and that does not sound like fun in my book!

To Walter and his team at Art Gallery Fabrics; I can always rely on you when I send last-minute emails asking for this and that—I know without fail that your amazing fabrics will be on my doorstep in two days. So thank you for being a great friend.

To the great team at Robert Kaufman Fabrics (www. robertkaufman.com); thank you for continuing to support my work.

To my new friends at Michael Miller, Andover, and Benartex; thank you for answering the random blind emails from me asking to work together. I look forward to working with you more and more.

To Bradley from Aurifil Threads; thank you for sending me all the threads I use for every part of the quilts. You are what holds it all together!

My favorite batting, the new Warm 100, comes from Lindsey at The Warm Company.

You can't make a quilt without cutting some fabric, and I rely on the support of Yvonne and the team at Olfa—they make the best rotary cutters and rulers around.

I would also like to thank my old friends at Quilt Now, Popular Patchwork, Love Patchwork & Quilting, Quilty, Modern Patchwork and so many more for their overwhelming support and understanding. I love being able to work with you all and hope we can continue to make amazing things together.

And finally, from the bottom of my heart, I would like to thank Penny and Anna from CICO Books for giving me this opportunity. Also a huge thank you to Marie Clayton; without her great editing, my misworded rambling instructions would never be suitable for print. Thank you for making me look good!